SIX
SIGMA
ON A BUDGET

Achieving More with Less Using the
PRINCIPLES of SIX SIGMA

Warren Brussee

D1444657

McGraw Hill

New York   Chicago   San Francisco   Lisbon   London
Madrid   Mexico City   Milan   New Delhi   San Juan
Seoul   Singapore   Sydney   Toronto

1 2 3 4 5 6 7 8 9 0   DOC/DOC   1 9 8 7 6 5 4 3 2 1 0

ISBN: 978-0-07-173675-6
MHID: 0-07-173675-1

This publication is designed to provide accurate and authoritative information in regard to the subject matter covered. It is sold with the understanding that the publisher is not engaged in rendering legal, accounting, or other professional service. If legal advice or other expert assistance is required, the services of a competent professional person should be sought.
    —*From a Declaration of Principles Jointly Adopted by a Committee of the American Bar Association and a Committee of Publishers and Associations*

McGraw-Hill books are available at special quantity discounts to use as premiums and sales promotions, or for use in corporate training programs. To contact a representative, please visit the Contact Us pages at www.mhprofessional.com.

This book is printed on acid-free paper

This book is dedicated to my grandchildren.
May they never forget those born and raised
without the gifts they have been given.

CONTENTS

PART 1 OVERVIEW

Chapter 1
General Six Sigma   3

Introduction   3
The History of Six Sigma   4
The Six Sigma Goal   5
Management's Role   5
Six Sigma Titles   5
Six Sigma Teams   6

Chapter 2
Measurements and Problem Solving   7

Metrics and Keeping Score   7
The DMAIC Problem-Solving Method   8

PART 2 NONSTATISTICAL SIX SIGMA TOOLS

Chapter 3
Customer-Driven Needs and Concerns   15

The Simplified QFD   15
Traditional QFDs   21
The Simplified FMEA   23
Traditional FMEAs   28

Chapter 4

Visual Assists   31

Fishbone Diagrams   31

Instructions for Fishbone Diagrams   32

Simplified Process Flow Diagrams   34

Instructions for Simplified Process Flow Diagrams   37

Visual Correlation Tests   40

PART 3 GETTING GOOD DATA

Chapter 5

Data and Samples   49

Types of Data   49

Data Discrimination   50

Collecting Samples   53

Average and Variation   58

Chapter 6

Simplified Gauge Verification   71

Checking for Gauge Error   73

Instructions for Simplified Gauge Verification   74

Example of Simplified Gauge Verification on Bearings   76

Gauge R&R   78

PART 4 PROBABILITY, PLOTS, AND STATISTICAL TESTS

Chapter 7

Data Overview   83

Probability   83

Data Plots and Distributions   92

Plotting Data   108

Chapter 8

Testing for Statistically Significant Change   115

Testing for Statistically Significant Change Using Variables Data   115

Using a Sample to Check for a Change versus a Population   124

Checking for a Statistically Significant Change between
Two Samples   133

Incidental Statistics Terminology Not Used in Preceding Tests   139

Testing for Statistically Significant Change Using
Proportional Data   140

Testing for Statistically Significant Change,
Nonnormal Distributions   150

PART 5 PROCESS CONTROL, DOEs, AND RSS TOLERANCES

Chapter 9

General and Focused Control   157

General Process Control   157

Traditional Control Charts   158

Simplified Control Charts   158

Chapter 10

Design of Experiments and Tolerance Analysis   163

Design of Experiments   163

Simplified DOEs   164

RSS Tolerances   165

Appendix: The Six Sigma Statistical Tool Finder Matrix   167

Glossary   169

Related Reading   173

Index   175

PART ONE

Overview

CHAPTER 1

General Six Sigma

INTRODUCTION

In a slow economy, companies no longer have the luxury of business as usual. Organizations must try to prevent quality issues, quickly identify and solve problems if they do occur, and drive down costs by increasing efficiencies. Six Sigma has proven its value in all these areas, and it is already in use at many large manufacturing companies.

However, businesses of all sizes and types can benefit from the use of Six Sigma. Accounting firms, service companies, stock brokers, grocery stores, charities, government agencies, suppliers of healthcare, and virtually any organization making a product or supplying a service can gain from Six Sigma use. The intent of this book is to broaden its use into these other areas.

In the healthcare field, for example, there is much controversy on how to control rising medical costs. Yet there are few hard statistics related to the success of competing medical treatments. The need for good data analysis in the healthcare field makes Six Sigma a natural fit. As one specific example, in the United States, eight billion dollars per year is spent on various prostate cancer treatments. The costs of the various treatment options range from $2,000 to well over $50,000.

Yet, according to a study by the Agency for Healthcare Research and Quality (February 4, 2008, U.S. Department of Health and Human Services Agency for Healthcare Research and Quality), no one treatment has been proven superior to the others. The agency also noted that there is a lack of good comparative studies. Dr. Jim Yong Kim, a physician and the president of Dartmouth College, reiterated this in an interview on *Bill Moyers Journal* (September 11, 2009). Dr. Kim said that work done at Dartmouth showed great variation in outcomes between various hospitals and doctors, and he suggested that healthcare professionals needed to learn from industry and start using processes like Six Sigma to improve and reduce the costs of health delivery.

Six Sigma experts often make Six Sigma complex and intimidating. But the basic Six Sigma concepts are quite simple. *Six Sigma on a Budget* makes the whole process of implementing Six Sigma easy. This book walks readers through detailed and applicable examples and problems that enable anyone with a high school level of math ability and access to Microsoft's *Excel* to quickly become proficient in Six Sigma. There is no reason to hire expensive Six Sigma experts or spend a large number of hours learning everything related to Six Sigma before beginning to apply this methodology. Aspects of Six Sigma can be implemented after reading just a few chapters of this book.

THE HISTORY OF SIX SIGMA

Motorola developed much of the Six Sigma methodology in the 1980s. Motorola was putting large numbers of transistors into their electronic devices and every transistor had to work or the device failed. So Motorola decided they needed a tighter quality criteria based on defects per million rather than the traditional defects-per-thousand measure. The initial quality goal for the Six Sigma methodology was no more than three defects per million parts.

Then, in the 1990s, Jack Welch, CEO of General Electric, popularized Six Sigma by dictating its use across the whole of GE. The resultant profit and quality gains GE touted caused Six Sigma to be implemented in many large corporations. The Six Sigma-generated savings claimed are $16 billion at Motorola, $800 million at Allied Signal, and $12 billion at GE in its first five years of use.

Lean manufacturing, a spin-off of traditional Six Sigma, got its start at Toyota in Japan. In lean Six Sigma, manufacturing costs are reduced by reducing lead time, reducing work-in-process, minimizing wasted motion, and optimizing material flow.

THE SIX SIGMA GOAL

The Six Sigma methodology uses a specific problem-solving approach and Six Sigma tools to improve processes and products. This methodology is data driven.

The original goal of the Six Sigma methodology was to reduce unacceptable products to no more than three defects per million parts. Currently in most companies the Six Sigma goal is to make product that satisfies the customer and minimizes supplier losses to the point that it is not cost effective to pursue tighter quality.

MANAGEMENT'S ROLE

Many Six Sigma books advise that Six Sigma can't be implemented without complete management commitment and the addition of dedicated Six Sigma personnel. This has been one of the criticisms of Six Sigma: that excessive time and money spent on Six Sigma can pull funds and manpower from other company needs. This book emphasizes that Six Sigma can be implemented for little cost and with little fanfare!

SIX SIGMA TITLES

The primary implementers of Six Sigma projects are called green belts. These project leaders are trained in all the common Six Sigma tools and work as team leaders on Six Sigma projects. Six Sigma black belts generally have a higher level of Six Sigma expertise and are proficient in Six Sigma specific software. Master black belts generally have management responsibility for the Six Sigma organization, especially if Six Sigma is set up as a separate organization.

Anyone completing *Six Sigma on a Budget* will have the same level of expertise as a traditional Six Sigma green belt. There is no need for black belts or master black belts.

SIX SIGMA TEAMS

Six Sigma teams are very fluid, with their composition based on a project's needs and the stage of the project. The most important factor on Six Sigma teams is that every area affected by a project be represented. This could include engineers, quality inspectors, people assembling or doing a task, people buying related materials or shipping product, and the customer.

WHAT WE HAVE LEARNED IN CHAPTER 1

- Motorola was the first large company to implement Six Sigma in the 1980s. Other large companies, like Allied Signal and GE, soon followed Motorola's lead.
- The Six Sigma methodology uses a specific problem-solving approach and select Six Sigma tools to improve processes and products.
- The initial Six Sigma quality goal was no more than three defects per million parts. A more realistic goal is to make a product good enough that it is not cost effective to pursue tighter quality.
- Anyone completing *Six Sigma on a Budget* will have the same level of expertise as a traditional Six Sigma green belt.

CHAPTER 2

Measurements and Problem Solving

METRICS AND KEEPING SCORE

In this section you will learn that when doing a Six Sigma project you must establish a performance baseline at the start of the project. This enables you to see where you are, in terms of defects, and to know if you have made an improvement with your Six Sigma work.

Metrics, the term used in quality control, refers to the system of measurement that gauges performance. There are many metrics used in industry related to quality. In this text we will use three of the most common metrics: DPM (defects per million), process sigma level, and DPMO (defects per million opportunities).

Defects per million (DPM) is the most common measurement of defect level, and it is the primary measurement used in this book. This metric closely relates to the bottom-line cost of defects, because it labels a part as being simply good or bad, with no indication as to whether a part is bad due to multiple defects or due to a single defect.

The process sigma level enables someone to project the DPM by analyzing a representative sample of a product. Also it enables some comparison of relative defect levels between different processes. Defects per million opportunities (DPMO) helps in identifying possible solutions because it identifies key problem areas rather than just labeling a part as bad. For example, defining a defect *opportunity* on a part requires identifying all the different defects that occur on the part, how many places on that part the defects can occur, and every production step that the product goes through that could cause one or more of the defects.

Suppose a glass part can have a crack or chip, both considered separate defects, occurring in any of three protrusions on the part. You identify two places in the process where the crack or chip could have occurred. This would be a total of 2 defects × 3 protrusions × 2 places = 12 opportunities for a defect. Assume that at the end of the production line we see protrusion cracks or chips on 10 percent of the glass parts. The defects per opportunity would be the 10 percent defect rate divided by the number of opportunities, or 0.1/12 = .008333. If we want to convert this to DPMO we must multiply the defects per opportunity by a million. This gives us a DPMO of 8,333.

The above example involves a manufactured product. However, DPMO applies to many other areas. For example, on looking at quantity errors made on phone orders, a person ordering a quantity of an item could make a mistake when stating the number he or she wants, the person receiving the information could misunderstand the caller, the wrong quantity could be mistakenly entered into the order computer, or the person filling the order could misread the order or just send the wrong quantity. This is five different opportunities for the error. If quantities were entered on two separate items, there would be 10 opportunities for error. If errors occur on 1 percent of orders involving two quantity inputs, the DPMO would be 0.01/10 ×1,000,000, which is a DPMO of 1,000.

THE DMAIC PROBLEM-SOLVING METHOD

What you will learn in this section is the DMAIC problem-solving approach used by green belts. This is a generic plan

DEFINITIONS

DMAIC: Define, Measure, Analyze, Improve, Control   This is the Six Sigma problem-solving approach used by green belts. It is the roadmap to be used on all projects and process improvements, with the Six Sigma tools applied as needed.

Define   This is the overall problem definition. This should be as specific and complete as possible.

Measure   Accurate and sufficient measurements and data are needed. Data are the essence of many Six Sigma projects.

Analyze   The measurements and data must be analyzed to see if they are consistent with the problem definition and to see if they identify a root cause. A problem solution is then identified.

Improve   Once a solution is identified, it must be implemented. The results must then be verified with independent data. Past data are seldom sufficient.

Control   A verification of control must be implemented. A robust solution (like a part change) will be easier to keep in control than a qualitative solution (like instructing an operator to run his process with different parameters).

that can be used on almost any type of problem. Which Six Sigma tools are used and what statistics are needed are dictated by each project. The Appendix has a Six Sigma statistical tool finder matrix that can be used in determining which Six Sigma tool is most helpful for each DMAIC step. As we learn to use each tool in the following chapters, we will refer back to its use in the DMAIC process.

Define the Problem

A problem is often initially identified very qualitatively, without much detail:

> "The customer is complaining that the quality of the motors has deteriorated."

> "The new personnel-attendance software program keeps crashing."

> "The losses on grinder 4 seem higher recently."

Before one can even think about possible solutions, the problem must be defined more specifically. Only then can meaningful measurements or data be collected. Here are the above examples after some additional definition:

> "More of the quarter-horsepower motors are failing the loading test beginning March 20."
>
> "The personnel-attendance software crashes several times per day when the number of absences exceeds 50."
>
> "The incidence of grinder 4 product being scrapped for small diameters has doubled in the last week."

Getting good problem definition may be as simple as talking to the customer. In this text there are several excellent tools for quantifying customer input. Often, however, the improved definition will require more effort. Some preliminary measurements may have to be taken to be sure that there even *is* a problem. It may be necessary to verify measurements and calculate sample sizes to be sure that you have valid and sufficient data.

In tight economic times, it is extremely critical to carefully and fully define a problem before attempting to solve it. Even with massive companywide training in Six Sigma, on one large Six Sigma project GE misinterpreted what the customer needed related to delivery times and spent months solving the wrong problem. GE went after improving the average delivery time; but the customer's issue was the relatively few deliveries that were extremely late. In this era of tight resources, this kind of misuse of time and manpower chasing the wrong problem is no longer acceptable.

Measure the Problem Process

Once the problem has been defined, it must be decided what additional measurements have to be taken to quantify it. Samples must be sufficient in number, random, and representative of the process we wish to measure.

Analyze the Data

Now we have to see what the data are telling us. We have to plot the data to understand the process character. We must decide if the problem as defined is *real* or just a random event without an assignable cause. If the event is random, we cannot look for a specific process change.

Improve the Process

Once we understand the root cause of the problem and have quantitative data, we identify solution alternatives. We then implement the chosen solution and verify the predicted results.

Control

Quality control data samples and measurement verification should be scheduled. Updated tolerances should reflect any change. A simplified control chart can be implemented if appropriate.

Using DMAIC

It is strongly recommended that *all* DMAIC steps be followed when problem solving. Remember, trying to fix a change that was implemented without first working through all the applicable steps may cause you to spend more time responding to the resultant problems than if you had taken the time to do it right!

The DMAIC roadmap is not only useful for problem troubleshooting; it also works well as a checklist when doing a project. In addition to any program management tool that is used to run a project, it is often useful to make a list of Six Sigma tools that are planned for each stage of the DMAIC process as the project progresses.

WHAT WE HAVE LEARNED IN CHAPTER 2

- When doing a Six Sigma project you have to establish a baseline. In this way you will be able to know if you made an improvement.
- Metrics are a system of measurements. In this text we use three metrics: defects per million (DPM), process sigma level, and defects per million opportunities (DPMO).
- The metric DPM most closely relates to the cost of defects, because it simply labels a part as being good or bad, with no indication as to whether a part is bad due to a single or multiple defects.
- The DMAIC (define, measure, analyze, improve, and control) process is the process roadmap Six Sigma green belts use to solve problems.

PART TWO

Nonstatistical Six Sigma Tools

CHAPTER 3

Customer-Driven Needs and Concerns

THE SIMPLIFIED QFD

Years ago, when travel money was plentiful and quality organizations were much larger, quality engineers were "deployed" to customers to rigorously probe the customers' needs. These engineers then created a series of quality function deployment (QFD) forms that transitioned those needs into a set of actions for the supplier.

Although this process worked, it was very expensive and time-consuming. Companies can no longer afford that. The simplified QFD described in this book accomplishes the same task in a condensed manner and at far less cost. This is extremely important in our current tight economic times. QFDs are one of the ways of hearing the voice of the customer (VOC), which is often referred to in lean Six Sigma.

What you will learn in this section is that what a customer really needs is often not truly understood during the design or change of a product, process, or service. Those doing a project often just assume that they understand the customer's wants and needs. A simplified QFD will minimize issues arising from this potential lack of understanding.

In Chapter 1, I suggested that healthcare costs could be reduced substantially with the rigorous application of Six

Sigma techniques. Patients and doctors should have valid comparative-effectiveness data to help them pick the best treatment options. If we could do a simplified QFD with a large number of doctors and their patients, I suspect that good data on treatment options would come out as a high need.

If you were limited to only one Six Sigma tool, you would use the simplified QFD. It is useful for any type of problem and should be used on every problem. It takes a relatively small amount of time and achieves buy-in from customers.

What is presented here is a simplified version of the QFDs likely to be presented in many Six Sigma books and classes. Some descriptions of the traditional QFDs and the rationale for the simplification are given later in this section. The simplified QFD is usually used in the Define or Improve steps of the DMAIC process. It converts customer needs into prioritized actions, which can then be addressed as individual projects. Here are some examples of how a QFD is used:

Manufacturing

Use the simplified QFD to get customer input as to their needs at the start of every new design or before any change in process or equipment.

New Product Development

Simplified QFDs are very effective in transitioning and prioritizing customer "wants" into specific items to be incorporated into a new product.

Sales and Marketing

Before any new sales initiative, do a simplified QFD, inviting potential customers, salespeople, advertisement suppliers, and others to give input.

Accounting and Software Development

Before developing a new program language or software package, do a simplified QFD. A customer's input is essential for a seamless implementation of the program.

Receivables

Do a simplified QFD on whether your approach on collecting receivables is optimal. Besides those directly involved in dealing with receivables, invite customers who are overdue on receivables to participate.

Insurance

Do a simplified QFD with customers to see what they look for to pick an insurance company or what it would take to make them switch.

The "customers" in the QFD include everyone who will touch the product, such as suppliers, production, packaging, shipping, sales, and end users. They are all influenced by any design or process change. Operators of equipment, service people, and implementers can be both customers and suppliers.

The most important step of doing any QFD is making sure that a large number of suppliers, operators, and customers contribute to the required QFD form. Most Six Sigma books say that this must be done in a massive meeting with everyone attending. Given tight budgets and time restraints, this is generally no longer possible. Nor is it required. E-mail and telephone calls are sufficient. Just make sure that every group affected by the project is involved. As you read the following, refer to the simplified QFD form in Figure 3-1 to see the application.

Instructions for Simplified QFDs

The simplified QFD form is a way of quantifying design options, always measuring these options against customer

FIGURE 3–1

Simplified QFD Form.
From Warren Brussee, *All About Six Sigma*.

QFD: License Plate Holder Option for Luxury Automobile

Ratings: 5 highest to 1 lowest (or negative number).
Numbers in parentheses are the result of multiplying
the customer need rating by the design item rating.

Customer Needs	Ratings	Metal Cast Rim	Plastic Cast Complete	Stamped Steel Rim	All Holes Already In	Optional Punched Holes	Gold/Silver Plating	Hex/Slotted Plastic Screws	Hex/Slotted Plated Steel Screws	Plastic Lens, Separate	Tempered-Glass Lens, Separate
Embossed Name	5	5 (25)	5 (25)	3 (15)	0 (0)	0 (0)	0 (0)	0 (0)	0 (0)	0 (0)	0 (0)
Place for Dealer Name	5	5 (25)	5 (25)	5 (25)	0 (0)	0 (0)	0 (0)	0 (0)	0 (0)	0 (0)	0 (0)
Must Hold All State Plates	5	5 (25)	5 (25)	5 (25)	5 (25)	5 (25)	0 (0)	0 (0)	0 (0)	0 (0)	0 (0)
Solid Feel	3	5 (15)	3 (9)	2 (6)	0 (0)	0 (0)	0 (0)	1 (3)	4 (12)	2 (6)	5 (15)
Gold or Silver Option	2	5 (10)	5 (10)	3 (6)	0 (0)	0 (0)	5 (10)	5 (10)	5 (10)	0 (0)	0 (0)
Easy to Install	4	3 (12)	5 (20)	3 (12)	5 (20)	3 (12)	0 (0)	5 (20)	3 (12)	3 (12)	2 (8)
Corrosion Resistant	4	3 (12)	5 (20)	2 (8)	0 (0)	0 (0)	3 (12)	5 (20)	3 (12)	4 (16)	5 (20)
Light Weight (for MPG)	1	1 (1)	4 (4)	5 (5)	0 (0)	0 (0)	0 (0)	5 (5)	2 (2)	5 (5)	1 (1)
Luxury Look	4	5 (20)	2 (8)	1 (4)	2 (8)	4 (16)	5 (20)	1 (4)	5 (20)	2 (8)	5 (20)
No Sharp Corners	5	4 (20)	5 (25)	2 (10)	4 (20)	2 (10)	0 (0)	5 (25)	3 (15)	5 (25)	2 (10)
Transparent Lens	4	0 (0)	3 (12)	0 (0)	0 (0)	0 (0)	0 (0)	0 (0)	0 (0)	3 (12)	5 (20)
Last 10 Years	5	4 (20)	4 (20)	3 (15)	0 (0)	0 (0)	3 (15)	5 (25)	4 (20)	3 (15)	5 (25)
Low Cost	2	1 (2)	5 (10)	4 (8)	5 (10)	2 (4)	1 (2)	5 (10)	3 (6)	4 (8)	2 (4)
Keep Appearance 10 Years	4	4 (16)	3 (12)	2 (8)	0 (0)	0 (0)	2 (8)	5 (20)	3 (12)	3 (12)	5 (20)
GROUPINGS TOTALS PRIORITIES		(203) **1**	(225)	(147)	(83) **3**	(67)	(67) **4**	(142) **2**	(121)	(119)	(143) **NA**

needs. The first step of doing the simplified QFD form is to make a list of the customer needs, with each being rated with a value of 1 to 5:

> 5 is a critical or a safety need; a need that must be satisfied.
>
> 4 is very important.
>
> 3 is highly desirable.
>
> 2 is nice to have.
>
> 1 is wanted if it's easy to do.

The customer needs and ratings are listed down the left-hand side of the simplified QFD form. Across the top of the simplified QFD form are potential actions to address the customer needs. Note that the customer needs are often expressed qualitatively (easy to use, won't rust, long life, etc.), whereas the design action items listed will be more specific (tabulated input screen, stainless steel, sealed roller bearings, etc.). Under each design action item and opposite each customer need, insert a value (1 to 5) to rate how strongly that design item addresses the customer need.

> 5 means it addresses the customer need completely.
>
> 4 means it addresses the customer need well.
>
> 3 means it addresses the customer need some.
>
> 2 means it addresses the customer need a little.
>
> 1 means it addresses the customer need very little.
>
> 0 or blank means it does not affect customer need.

A negative number means it is detrimental to that customer need. (A negative number is not that unusual, since a solution to one need sometimes hurts another need.)

Put the rating in the upper half of the block beneath the design item and opposite the need. Then multiply the design rating times the value assigned to the corresponding customer need value. Enter this result into the lower half of the square under the design action item rating. These values will have a possible range of −25 to +25.

Once all the design items are rated against every customer need, the values in the lower half of the boxes under each design item are summed and entered into the Totals row at the bottom of the sheet. The solutions with the highest values are usually the preferred design solutions to address the customer needs.

Once these totals are reviewed, someone may feel that something is awry and want to go back and review some ratings or design solutions. This second (or third) review is extremely valuable. Also the customer needs rated 5 should have priority.

Potential actions to address the customer's needs may require some brainstorming. One of the tools that can assist in this brainstorming is the fishbone diagram, which is discussed in Chapter 4.

In the simplified QFD form, near the bottom, design action items are grouped when only one of several options can be done. In this case there would be only one priority number assigned within the group. In Figure 3-1, the priorities showed that the supplier should cast a plastic license plate cover with built-in plastic lens. This precludes the need for a separate lens, which is why the NA (not applicable) is shown in the separate lens grouping.

The form can be tweaked to make it more applicable to the product, process, or service it is addressing. The importance is in getting involvement from as many affected parties as possible and using the simplified QFD form to influence design direction.

The simplified QFD form should be completed for all new designs or process modifications. The time and cost involved will be more than offset by making the correct decisions up front rather than having to make multiple changes later.

The simplified QFD form shown in Figure 3-1 can be done by hand or in Excel. In any case, the building and rating should be sent to every contributing party on a regular basis as the form is being developed.

Note that the QFDs shown in this book are a lot neater and more organized than they would appear as the QFDs are being developed. As inputs are collected, needs and potential actions may not be logically grouped, nor will they necessarily be in prioritized order. A more organized QFD, such as shown in Figure 3-1, will occur later, when it is formalized.

Don't get hung up on trying to do the form on a computer if that is not your expertise. A simplified QFD done neatly by hand with copies sent to all participants is fully acceptable. With current time restraints, none of us have time to spend on frustrating niceties.

Case Study: Options for Repairing a High-Speed Machine

A high-speed production machine had a large number of molds that opened and closed as they traveled along the machine. At one location in the molds' journey, the molds would sometimes contact the product, causing an unacceptable mark in that product. This was caused by wear in the mechanism that carried the molds. The manufacturing plant wanted to see if there was a way to eliminate this problem without an expensive rebuilding of the mechanism that carried the molds. Figure 3-2 shows the QFD that was done on this issue.

One of the engineers at the QFD meeting came up with a seemingly clever idea to use magnets to hold the molds open at the problem area on the machine. This was the chosen option, which was far less expensive than the baseline approach of a rebuild.

This project is discussed further in the next section on FMEAs.

TRADITIONAL QFDs

A traditional QFD, as taught in most classes and books on Six Sigma, is likely to be one of the following:

The first and most likely is a QFD consisting of four forms. The first form in this QFD is the "House of Quality." This form covers product planning and competitor benchmarking. The second form is "Part Deployment," which shows key part characteristics. The third form shows "Critical-to-Customer Process Operations." The fourth is "Production Planning."

FIGURE 3-2

QFD.
From Warren Brussee, *All About Six Sigma.*

Ratings: 5 highest to 1 lowest (or negative number). Numbers in parentheses are the result of multiplying the customer need rating by the design item rating.								
		Design Items						
Customer Needs	**Ratings**	Rebuild Current Design	Rebuild Lighter Design	Increase Cam Opening Distance	Machine-Off Mold Contact Area	Use Air to Hold Molds	Use Vacuum to Hold Molds	Use Magnets to Hold Molds
Inexpensive	4	2 (8)	1 (4)	3 (12)	4 (16)	3 (12)	2 (8)	5 (20)
Quick	2	2 (4)	1 (2)	3 (6)	3 (6)	5 (10)	2 (4)	5 (10)
Low Risk	4	5 (20)	4 (16)	1 (4)	1 (4)	1 (4)	0 (0)	5 (20)
Quality OK	5	5 (25)	5 (25)	1 (5)	1 (5)	1 (5)	4 (20)	5 (25)
Permanent Fix	3	4 (12)	5 (15)	1 (3)	1 (3)	3 (9)	3 (9)	5 (15)
Easy	2	2 (4)	1 (2)	2 (4)	4 (8)	3 (6)	4 (8)	5 (10)
Little Downtime	3	2 (6)	1 (3)	3 (9)	4 (12)	4 (12)	4 (12)	5 (15)
TOTALS		(79)	(67)	(43)	(54)	(58)	(61)	(115)
PRIORITIES		2	3					1

Two other possible QFDs are the "Matrix of Matrices," consisting of 30 matrices, and the "Designer's Dozen," consisting of 12 QFD matrices.

Needless to say, these traditional QFDs take much more time and effort than the simplified QFD. Meetings to complete the traditional QFDs generally take at least four times as long as the meetings required for the simplified QFD on an equivalent project.

If the QFD form is too complex, or the meeting to do the form takes too long, people lose focus and the quality of the input diminishes. The simplified QFD, as taught in this book, is designed to get needed input with the minimum of hassle.

THE SIMPLIFIED FMEA

What we will learn in this section is that on any project there can be collateral damage to areas outside the project. A simplified failure modes and effects analysis (FMEA) will reduce this likelihood. A simplified FMEA will generate savings largely through cost avoidance. It is usually used in the Define or Improve steps of the DMAIC process.

Traditional FMEAs, as taught in most Six Sigma classes and books, are complex, time-consuming, and expensive to do. Not so with a simplified FMEA, which is used with the simplified QFD. Both Six Sigma tools should be used on every project, process change, or new development. It may be tempting to skip doing the simplified FMEA given the tight resource environment, but as you will see in the case study later in this section, the simplified FMEA can save a lot of grief. A brief discussion of traditional FMEAs and the reason for the simplification comes later in this section.

Note that the simplified FMEA format is very similar to that used for the simplified QFD. This is intentional, since the goal is to use both on every new product or change. Since many of the same people will be involved in both the QFD and the FMEA, the commonality of both forms simplifies the task, saving time and money. A simplified FMEA uses input on concerns to address collateral risks. Here are some examples:

Manufacturing

Before implementing any new design, process, or change, do a simplified FMEA. An FMEA converts qualitative concerns into specific actions. You need input on what possible negative outcomes could occur.

Sales and Marketing

A change in a sales or marketing strategy can affect other products or cause an aggressive response by a competitor. A simplified FMEA is one way to make sure that all the possible ramifications are understood and addressed.

Accounting and Software Development

The introduction of a new software package or a different accounting procedure sometimes causes unexpected problems for those affected. A simplified FMEA will reduce unforeseen problems.

Receivables

How receivables are handled can affect future sales with a customer. A simplified FMEA will help to understand concerns of both the customer and internal salespeople and identify approaches that minimize future sales risks while reducing overdue receivables.

Insurance

The balance between profits and servicing customers on insurance claims is dynamic. A simplified FMEA helps keep people attuned to the risks associated with any actions under consideration.

A simplified FMEA is a method of anticipating things that can go wrong even if a proposed project, task, or modification is completed as expected. Often a project generates so much support and enthusiasm that it lacks a healthy amount of skeptics, especially in regard to any negative effects that the project may have on things not directly related to it. There are usually multiple ways to solve a problem, and the best solution is often the one that has the least risk to other parts of the process. The emphasis in a simplified FMEA is to identify affected components or issues downstream, or on related processes that may have issues caused by the program.

For example, a simplified QFD on healthcare would likely show that good data on treatment options is a high need. Equally, an FMEA on healthcare would likely result in a list of possible side effects as being a high concern, even if the treatment option were judged as being successful in its primary medical goal.

Just as in the simplified QFD, the critical step is getting input from everyone who has anything to do with the project. These people could be machine operators, customers, shipping personnel, or even suppliers. These inputs can come via e-mail, phone calls, and so on. There is no reason to have the expense of massive meetings as is advised in most Six Sigma classes and books.

Instructions for Simplified FMEAs

The left-hand column of the simplified FMEA form (Figure 3-3) is a list of possible things that could go wrong, assuming that the project is completed as planned. The first task doing an FMEA is to generate this list of concerns. On this list could be unforeseen issues on other parts of the process, safety issues, environmental concerns, negative effects on existing similar products, or even employee problems. These will be rated in importance:

5 is a safety or critical concern.

4 is a very important concern.

3 is a medium concern.

2 is a minor concern.

1 is a matter for discussion to see if it is an issue.

Across the top of the simplified FMEA is a list of solutions to address the concerns that have been identified. Below each potential solution and opposite the concern, each response item is rated on how well it addresses the concern:

5 means it addresses the concern completely.

4 means it addresses the concern well.

3 means it addresses the concern satisfactorily.

2 means it addresses the concern somewhat.

1 means it addresses the concern very little.

0 or a blank means it does not affect the concern.

A negative number means the solution actually makes the concern worse.

FIGURE 3-3

A simplified FMEA.
From Warren Brussee, *All About Six Sigma*.

FMEA: Magnets Holding Tooling Open					
Ratings: 5 highest to 1 lowest (or negative number). Numbers in parentheses are the result of multiplying the customer concern rating by the solution item rating.				Solutions	
Concerns	**Ratings**	Mount a Degausser after Magnets	Mount ProxSwitch and Use Breakaway Mounts	Use Electric Magnets; Adjust Current and Turn Off to Clean	Check with Pacemaker Mfg: Shield If Required
Tooling Will Become Magnetized	4	4 (16)	0 (0)	0 (0)	0 (0)
Caught Product Will Hit Magnets, Wreck Machine	5	0 (0)	3 (15)	0 (0)	0 (0)
Magnets Will Get Covered with Metal Filings	2	2 (4)	0 (0)	3 (6)	0 (0)
One Operator Has a Heart Pacemaker	5	? (?)	0 (0)	0 (0)	? (?)
Magnets Will Cause Violent Tooling Movement	2	0 (0)	0 (0)	3 (6)	0 (0)
TOTALS PRIORITIES		(?)	(15)	(12)	(?)

Enter this value in the upper half of the block, beneath the solution item and opposite the concern. After these ratings are complete, multiply each rating times the concern value on the left. Enter this product in the lower half of each box. Add all the values in the lower half of the boxes in each column and enter the sum in the Totals row indicated near the bottom of the form. These are then prioritized, with the highest value being the primary consideration for implementation.

As in the simplified QFD, these summations are only a point of reference. It is appropriate to reexamine the concerns and ratings.

Case Study: A Potential Life-Saving Simplified FMEA on Repairing a High-Speed Machine

The subject for this case study was already covered earlier, where a simplified QFD was developed. On page 26 is the simplified FMEA (Figure 3-3) that was done after the simplified QFD was completed.

A high-speed production machine was experiencing wear issues. This wear caused the tooling to have too much play, which allowed it to rub against the product at one specific location on the machine, causing quality issues. The cost of rebuilding the machine was very high, so the manufacturing plant wanted other options of solving this problem.

An engineer came up with what seemed like an ingenious solution. Powerful magnets would be mounted just outboard of the machine at the problem area, near the steel tooling. These magnets would attract and hold open the steel tooling as it went by, eliminating the chance of the tooling rubbing against the product. This solution was especially attractive because it would be inexpensive, easy to do, and would solve the problem completely. The initial engineering study found no show-stoppers in regard to installing the magnets. Bench tests with actual magnets and tooling indicated that it would work extremely well.

Everyone was anxious to implement this project, since all the parts were readily available and they would be easy to install on the machine for a test. But, a requirement of the Six Sigma process was to first do a simplified FMEA to see if this solution could cause other issues. So, a group of production engineers, foremen, operators, maintenance people, and quality technicians did a simplified FMEA.

Most of the concerns that surfaced had obvious solutions. However, the input that one of the machine operators had a heart pacemaker was a complete surprise, and no one had any idea of how the magnets would affect the pacemaker.

On following up with the pacemaker manufacturer, it was discovered that even the pacemaker manufacturer was not sure how their device would be affected by the powerful magnets. They did say, however, that they had serious reservations. The pacemaker manufacturer was not interested in testing one of their pacemakers in their own labs using one of the proposed magnets. They wanted no involvement whatsoever!

Other options were discussed, like reassigning the operator to a different machine. But all of those options raised additional issues, such as union issues on the reassignment. The machine operator had to be free to access all areas of the machine, so a barrier physically isolating the area around the magnets was not an option.

At this point, the option of using magnets was abandoned because there seemed to be no way to eliminate the possible risk to the operator with the pacemaker. The machine had to be rebuilt despite the high cost.

Without the simplified FMEA, the project would have been implemented, with some real risk that the operator could have been hurt or even lost his life.

Although the preceding case study is more dramatic than most, seldom is a simplified FMEA done without uncovering some issue that was previously unknown.

TRADITIONAL FMEAS

As mentioned earlier, the simplified FMEA is less complex than the traditional FMEA normally taught in Six Sigma. A traditional FMEA requires the people doing the forms to identify each potential failure event, and then for each of these events to identify the failure mode, consequences of a failure, potential cause of the failure, severity of a failure, current design controls to prevent a failure, failure detection likelihood, expected frequency of a failure, impact of the failure, risk priority, recommended action to prevent the failure, and the likelihood of that action succeeding. The traditional FMEA requires far more forms and takes much more time than the simplified FMEA. Having sat through many traditional FMEAs, my observation is that by the time they were complete, people were just trying to get them done without worrying too much about the quality of the inputs.

WHAT WE HAVE LEARNED IN CHAPTER 3

- The simplified QFD is usually used in the Define or Improve steps of the DMAIC process. The simplified QFD should be used on every new product or product/process change.
- A simplified FMEA is usually used in the Define or Improve steps of DMAIC. A simplified FMEA emphasizes identifying concerns in other affected areas and prioritizing potential solutions to these concerns.

Visual Assists

FISHBONE DIAGRAMS

It is critical to identify and examine all the possible causes for a problem. This section explains how a fishbone diagram is used to assist in this task.

The fishbone diagram is used primarily in the Define, Analyze, and Improve steps of the DMAIC process. It helps identify which input variables should be studied further and gives focus to the analysis.

Fishbone diagrams are extremely useful and work well when used in conjunction with QFDs. In fact, sometimes they must be used before doing the QFD to assist in generating the list of customer "wants."

The purpose of a fishbone diagram is to identify all the input variables that could be causing a problem and then look for cause-and-effect relationships. Once we have a complete list of input variables, we identify the critical few key process input variables (KPIVs) to measure and further investigate.

Here are some examples of how to use a fishbone diagram to identify possible key process inputs that may have a cause-and-effect relationship on the problem being studied.

Manufacturing

Do a fishbone diagram to list all the important input variables related to a problem. Highlight the KPIVs for further study. This focus minimizes sample collection and data analysis.

Sales and Marketing

For periods of unusually low sales, use a fishbone diagram to identify possible causes of the low sales. The KPIVs enable identification of probable causes and often lead to possible solutions.

Accounting and Software Development

Use a fishbone diagram to identify the possible causes of unusual accounting or computer issues. The people in these areas respond well to this type of analysis.

Receivables

Identify periods of higher-than-normal delinquent receivables. Then use a fishbone diagram to try to understand the underlying causes.

Insurance

Look for periods of unusual claim frequency. Then do a fishbone diagram to understand underlying causes. This kind of issue usually has a large number of potential causes; the fishbone diagram enables screening to the critical few.

INSTRUCTIONS FOR FISHBONE DIAGRAMS

In fishbone diagrams, the specific problem of interest is the "head" of the fish. Then there are six "bones" on the fish on which we list input variables that affect the problem head.

Each bone has a category of input variables that should be listed. Separating the input variables into six different categories, each with its own characteristics, triggers us to make sure that no input variable is missed. The six categories are measurements, materials, men, methods, machines, and environment. (Some people remember these as the "five M's and one E.") The six categories are what make the fishbone more effective than a single-column list of all the input variables.

Most Six Sigma classes and books specify that the input variables on a fishbone should come from a group of "experts" working together in one room. With our current economic environment, getting everyone together in a meeting is not always possible. However, it is possible to do this process on the telephone, using e-mail to regularly send updated versions of the fishbone diagram to all the people contributing. Figure 4-1 is an abbreviated example of a fishbone diagram done on the problem "shaft diameter error."

FIGURE 4-1

Fishbone diagram.
From Warren Brussee, *Statistics for Six Sigma Made Easy.*

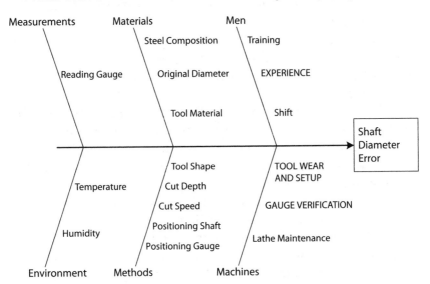

After listing all the input variables, the same team of experts should pick the two or three key process input variables (KPIVs) they feel are most likely to be the culprits. Those are highlighted in boldface and capital letters on the fishbone diagram in Figure 4-1.

There are software packages that enable someone to fill in the blanks of standardized forms for the fishbone diagram. However, other than for the sake of neatness, doing them by hand does just as well.

As you will see later in the book, the fishbone diagram is the recommended tool to identify what should be sampled in a process and to know what variables need to be kept in control during the sampling process. Without the kind of cause-and-effect analysis the fishbone diagram supports, the sampling will likely be less focused, take more time, and be fraught with error.

SIMPLIFIED PROCESS FLOW DIAGRAMS

In this section you will learn how to use a simplified process control diagram to identify and examine all the possible causes for a problem. A process control diagram can be used with a fishbone diagram to help identify the key process input variables.

This section gets into many areas of lean Six Sigma, where reducing lead time, reducing work-in-process, minimizing wasted motion, optimizing work area design, and streamlining material flow are some of the techniques used to reduce manufacturing costs. Both lean and traditional Six Sigma use a simplified process flow diagram to assist in identifying quality and cost issues. Both lean and traditional Six Sigma are very timely given the tight economic and competitive market we are in.

Of special interest in traditional Six Sigma is noting locations in the process where inspection or quality sorting takes place or where process data are collected. By looking at data from these positions you may see evidence of a change or a problem. This helps bring focus to the problem area.

Of special interest to lean Six Sigma is noting where product assembly, transfer, handling, accumulation, or transport occurs. Not only are these areas of potential cost savings, but many of these areas of excess handling and inventory are problem sources and delay timely response to an issue.

Lean manufacturing got its start at Toyota in Japan; but now U.S. companies are reexamining their processes using lean Six Sigma. As reported in *The Wall Street Journal* ("Latest Starbucks Buzzword: 'Lean' Japanese Techniques," by Julie Jargon, August 4, 2009), Starbucks is one of these companies.

Starbucks may seem like at odd place to be using this tool, but Starbucks is very sensitive to how long a customer must wait to be served. Customers will walk out if they feel that the wait is excessive. In applying lean techniques, according to the article, even a well-run Starbucks store was able to cut its average wait time. The position and means of storage of every element used to make drinks was analyzed to minimize wasted motion. The position and storage of all their food items was similarly examined. In this way, service time was reduced, along with wait time.

The traditional process flow diagram for Six Sigma shows steps in the process, with no relative positions or time between these steps. A lean Six Sigma process flow diagram gives a more spatial representation, so time and distance relationships are better understood.

Simplified process flow diagrams are used primarily in the Define, Analyze, and Improve steps of the DMAIC process. Here are some examples.

Manufacturing

The simplified process flow diagram will focus an investigation by identifying where or when in the process KPIVs could have affected the problem. Of special interest is where data is collected in the process, queuing occurs, or a product is assembled or transferred.

Sales and Marketing

A simplified process flow diagram will assist in identifying whether the cause of low sales is regional, personnel, or some other factor.

Accounting and Software Development

A simplified process flow diagram will help pinpoint the specific problem areas in a system or program. This knowledge simplifies the debug process. Software developers are very familiar with this process.

Receivables

Identify periods when delinquent receivables are higher than normal. A simplified process flow diagram may help in designing procedures, like discounts for early payment, to minimize the problem. Improved forms and computer input procedures can reduce the manpower required to address delinquent payments.

Insurance

Identify periods of unusual frequency of claims. A simplified process flow diagram may assist in identifying the changed claims period versus a normal claims period.

A simplified process flow diagram works well when used in conjunction with a fishbone diagram. It can further screen the KPIVs that were already identified in the fishbone, minimizing where you will have to take additional samples or data.

There are software packages that enable users to fill in the blanks of standardized forms for a process flow diagram. However, other than for the sake of neatness, doing them by hand does just as well.

INSTRUCTIONS FOR SIMPLIFIED PROCESS FLOW DIAGRAMS

A process flow diagram shows the relationships among the steps in a process or the components in a system, with arrows connecting all of the elements and showing the sequence of activities. Some texts and software for traditional process flow diagrams use additional geometrical shapes to differentiate between different process functions. I choose to keep it simple, only emphasizing where assembly, transfer, measurements, or quality judgments are made. This makes it easier for people who are not familiar with the traditional process flow symbols to use these forms.

When doing a simplified process flow diagram for lean Six Sigma, you will show relative distance and time between process steps, and, if desired, numerically show actual distance, time intervals for product flow, and inventory builds. The intent would be to identify areas where handling and process time can be reduced. In lean Six Sigma you want to be able to separate meaningful work from wasted time and motion. This wasted time and motion could include searching for components which perhaps would be easier to access if they were in color-coded bins. Ideally, a person's efforts would stay the same, or be reduced, while more product or services are performed due to improved process flow and efficiency. Sometimes, a person's or product's movements are so elaborate that the map that is developed is called a "spaghetti map." But, no matter what it is called, it is a process flow diagram.

Figure 4-2 shows a simplified process flow diagram for use in a traditional Six Sigma project.

Just as with the fishbone diagram, the simplified process flow diagram is not limited to uses related to solving problems in a manufacturing process or to a physical flow. The flow could be related to time or process steps, not just place.

FIGURE 4−2

A simplified process flow diagram, shaft machining.
From Warren Brussee, *Statistics for Six Sigma Made Easy.*

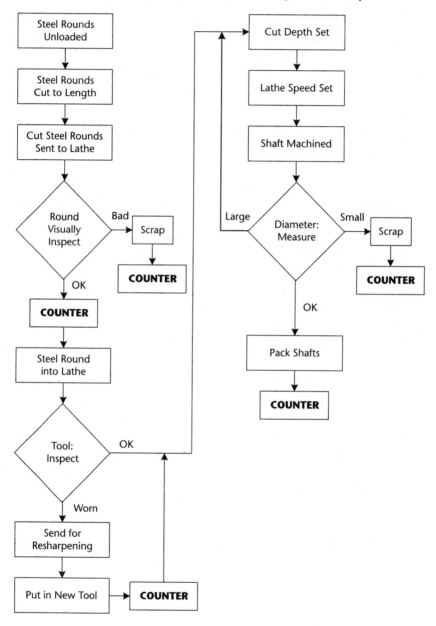

Case Study: Excess Material Handling

In a lean Six Sigma project, process flow charts showed that, in a manufacturing plant that ran 24 hours per day, the day shift had different product flow than the other shifts. On trying to understand why, it was found that the quality engineer insisted on being the final decision maker on the resolution of any product that was put into quality hold by the online quality checks. On the day shift, the quality engineer went to the held product and made a timely decision based on the inspection data. This caused the product to be either reinspected by day shift or sent to the warehouse. On the other shifts, the held product was taken to the warehouse until the next day shift when the quality engineer would review the data. Any product that the engineer deemed bad enough to require reinspection had to then be removed from the warehouse and taken to an inspection station. This caused extra handling of the off-shift product that required reinspection.

Once this practice was brought to the attention of management, the quality engineer was asked to document how he made the decision to reinspect or ship, and then the shift foremen were trained in this task. Also the day shift inspectors were distributed to the off-shifts so any held product could be reinspected in a timely manner.

This change reduced material handling, enabling the reduction of one material handler on day shift. But even more importantly, the reinspection on the off-shifts gave the shifts quicker feedback on any quality issues they had. This helped improve the off-shifts' overall product quality, reducing the quantity of held product requiring reinspection. This improved the overall profitability for the plant.

An issue to keep in mind when implementing lean Six Sigma is the legacy of scientific management, or Taylorism, that was developed in the late-19th and early-20th centuries. Taylorism emphasized using precise work procedures broken down into discrete motions to increase efficiency and to decrease waste through careful study of an individual at work. Over the years, this process has at times included time and motion study and other methods to improve managerial control over employee work practices. However, these scientific management methods have sometimes led to ill feelings from employees who felt as if they had been turned into automatons whose jobs had been made rote with little intellectual stimulation. Casual work attitudes on some assembly lines are one manifestation of this issue. Although lean Six

Sigma implementers will be quick to point out how what they do is different than those earlier approaches to efficiency, there are workers who are suspicious of any attempt to optimize work practices.

Probably the most effective way to minimize conflict during lean Six Sigma projects is to make sure communication with everyone involved is frank and open, with the emphasis being to eliminate boring and wasted tasks that do not add to job satisfaction. These improvements generally lead to improved productivity and quality without generating employee animosity. Also, when improving a work center, which includes optimizing parts placement, it is wise to be sure that an FMEA is done before the actual change is made to reduce unforeseen problems.

VISUAL CORRELATION TESTS

Visual correlation tests are another way to discover the key process input variables that may have caused a change in a process or product. Visual correlation tests are straightforward and only require collecting data, doing plots of that data, and then visually looking for correlations.

In some Six Sigma classes, regression analysis is used to identify these correlations. A mathematical curve is fit to a set of data, and techniques are used to measure how well the data fit these curves. The resultant curves are then used to test for correlations.

Regression analysis is generally not friendly to those who are not doing that kind of analysis almost daily. Thankfully, most Six Sigma work can be done without regression analysis by using visual examination of the data and their related graphs. Visual correlation tests are used primarily in the Define, Analyze, and Improve steps of the DMAIC process.

Something changed in a process or product and we would like to discover the KPIVs that caused it. Time and position are our most valued friends in doing the analysis. Following are some examples.

Manufacturing

Construct a time plot showing when a problem first appeared or when it comes and goes. Do similar time plots of the KPIVs to see if a change in any of those variables coincides with the timing of the problem change. If one or more correlate, do a controlled test to establish cause and effect for each correlated KPIV.

Sales and Marketing

For periods of unusually low sales activity, construct a time plot showing when the low sales started and stopped. Do similar time plots of the KPIVs to see if a change in any of those variables coincides with the low sales period. If so, do a controlled test to establish cause and effect for that KPIV.

Accounting and Software Development

Construct a time plot of unusual accounting or computer issues. Do similar time plots of the KPIVs to see if a change in any of those variables coincides with the issues. If one or more do, run a controlled test to establish cause and effect of each correlated KPIV.

Receivables and Insurance

Identify periods of higher than normal delinquent receivables or unusual claim frequency. Then construct a time plot of the problem and the related KPIVs. For any variable that shows coincident change, check for cause and/or effect with controlled tests.

Instructions for Correlation Tests

First isolate when and where the problem change took place. Do this by doing a time plot or position plot of every measurement of the process or product that is indicative of the change. These plots often define the time and/or position of the start/end of the change to a very narrow range. If the amount of change indicated by the plot is large compared to other data changes before and after the incidence and the timing corresponds to the observed problem recognition, it is generally worthwhile to check further for correlations.

The next thing to do is to look for correlations with input variables, using graphs of historical data. If the KPIVs are not already known, we must do a fishbone diagram or a process flow diagram to identify them. Do time plots or position plots of every KPIV, centering on the previously defined problem time period or position. Any input variable that changed at nearly the same time or position as the problem is suspect.

When there are multiple time and/or position agreements of change between the problem and an input variable, then do controlled tests where everything but the suspicious variable is kept constant. In this way, cause-and-effect relationships can be established.

If more than one KPIV changed, there could be an interaction between these variables, but usually one KPIV will stand out. Looking at extended time periods will often rule out input variables that do not correlate consistently.

Numerical methods to test for statistically significant change will be covered in Chapter 8. However, if there are multiple time agreements on changes between the problem and a KPIV, these extra tests are often not needed. In any case, controlled tests will have to be run to prove a true cause and effect between the suspect KPIV and the problem. If we cannot make the problem come and go by changing the suspect KPIV, then we have not identified the correct KPIV.

Figure 4-3 shows simplified plots of a problem and the KPIVs (A, B, and C). This visual check is very easy and often obvious, once plots of the problem and the KPIVs are compared with one another.

The B variable certainly looks suspicious, given that it had a change in the same time interval as the problem, matching both the beginning and end of the time period. As

FIGURE 4-3

Key process input variables.
From Warren Brussee, *All About Six Sigma.*

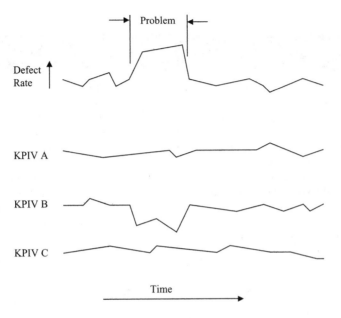

a first test, expand the time of the data for both the process defect rate and the B variable to see if this change agreement is truly as unique and correlated as it appears in the Figure 4-3 limited data. If, in the expanded data, either the defect appeared without the change in the suspect KPIV or the KPIV changed without a related defect change, then the suspect KPIV is likely not correctly identified. Remember, however, that this test will never be definitive. It will only hint—albeit strongly—at the cause. A test set up to control all possible variables (except for the B variable in Figure 4-3) will be required. We would intentionally change the B variable as shown in the plot in Figure 4-3 and see if the problem responds similarly. Only then have we truly established a cause-and-effect relationship.

When time plots of variables are compared to the change we are studying, it is important that any inherent time shift be incorporated. For example, if a raw material is put into a storage bin with three days previous inventory, this three-day delay must be incorporated when looking for a correlation of that raw material to the process.

TIP
Showing cause and effect

Correlation doesn't prove cause and effect. It just shows that two or more things happened to change at the same time or at the same position. There have been infamous correlations (stork sightings versus birth rates) that were just coincidental or had other explanations (people kept their houses warmer as the birth of a baby became imminent and the heat from the fireplaces attracted the storks).

To show true cause and effect, you must run controlled tests where only the key test input variable is changed (no additional fireplace heat at the time of births) and its effect measured (did the stork sightings still increase?). Normally, historical data can't be used to prove cause and effect because the data are too "noisy" and other variables are not being controlled.

Case Study: Incorrect Cause

A glass container was heated to extremely high temperatures in an indexing machine, and it was critical that the glass "softened" at a specific position on this machine. The people running this indexing heating device had historically complained that the glass containers softened at varying positions on the machine, hurting the final product quality.

It was believed that the cause of this problem was large variation in the wall thickness of each container. This was not a new problem and over the years the tolerances had been reduced on the wall thickness variation. These tolerances were now so tight that large losses were occurring in the supplier plant. Because the complaints continued, however, a major project was started to further reduce the wall variation within each container.

To find out how critical the variation in wall thickness was, the project team selected a large group of containers with different levels of wall thickness variation. These containers were then run on the indexing heating machine, and those with large variations were compared to containers with little individual wall variation. Plotting the machine softening positions of the containers with different degrees of wall variation, the project team saw no difference between the groups.

The historical belief that the wall thickness variation within each container was causing the container to soften at different positions was apparently wrong.

A search was started to find the correct KPIV that influenced the position at which the glass softened. Looking at periods of time when the customer complaints were highest versus times when the complaints were reduced, one of the KPIVs found to correlate was the average wall thickness of each container, not the wall variation within each container. When a test was run with containers grouped with others having similar average wall thicknesses, each container softened consistently at a given position on the indexing machine no matter what the individual wall variation. Results from additional tests, done in different plants on similar machines with the other variables in control, supported the cause-and-effect finding.

Visually checking for correlations on plotted data of wall variation versus the softening position on the indexing machine triggered the realization that container wall variation was not the culprit. No visual correlation was seen. Equally, there was a visual correlation between average wall thickness and the softening position.

This subtle finding that the average wall thickness was the key process input variable changed the way the container was manufactured. This saved the container manufacturer $400,000 per year. It also saved the production plants running the indexing machines $700,000 per year through better yields.

WHAT WE HAVE LEARNED IN CHAPTER 4

- The fishbone diagram is used primarily in the Define, Analyze, and Improve steps of the DMAIC process. The purpose of a fishbone diagram is to have experts identify all the input variables that could be causing the problem of interest, prioritize them, and then look for a cause-and-effect relationship.

- Simplified process flow diagrams are used primarily in the Define, Analyze, and Improve steps of the DMAIC process. A simplified process flow diagram will help pinpoint an area in which efforts should be concentrated.

- Correlation tests are used primarily in the Define, Analyze, and Improve steps of the DMAIC process. Something changed in a process or product and the goal is to discover the key process input variable that caused it.

PART THREE

Getting Good Data

CHAPTER 5

Data and Samples

TYPES OF DATA

All the statistics we use in Six Sigma draw on only two types of data: variables and proportional. In this chapter we show how to determine which type of data you have and discuss the advantages of each.

Variables Data

Variables data are normally related to measurements expressed as decimals. This type of data can theoretically be measured to whatever degree of accuracy desired, the only limitations being the measuring device and the decimal places to which you collect the data. This is why variables data are sometimes called *continuous data*.

Proportional Data

Proportional data are always ratios or probabilities. Proportional data are often expressed as decimals, but these decimals are the ratios of two numbers; they are not based on physical measurements. Proportional data are either ratios of attributes (good/bad, good/total, yes/no, and so on), or ratios of discreet or stepped numerical values.

For statistical analysis, variables data are preferred over proportional data because variables data allow us to make decisions using fewer samples.

DATA DISCRIMINATION

Some data need interpretation to determine if the data can be analyzed as variables. The following example shows how this determination can be made.

Below are individual ages collected from a group of people aged 50 to 55. Assume that these data are going to be used in a study of the incidence of a disease.

53.2	54.5
54.1	54.8
50.2	54.2
54.3	53.4
51.3	52.3
55.0	53.4
52.7	

Since the data were collected in units equal to tenths of a year, there is good discrimination of the data versus the five-year study period. Good discrimination means that the data steps are small compared to the five-year range being studied. These data have measurement steps of tenths of a year because the data were collected and displayed to one-decimal-point resolution.

Rule of Thumb on Variables Data Discrimination

On variables data, the measurement resolution should be sufficient to give at least 10 steps within the range of interest. For example, if data are collected on a part with a 0.050-inch tolerance, the data measurement steps should be no larger than 0.005 inch to be able to analyze that data as variables.

In the example, because the ages are displayed to the first decimal point, there are 50 discrimination steps in the five-year study period (5.0 divided by 0.1), which is greater than the 10-step minimum rule of thumb.

Let's suppose that the same data had been collected as ages 53, 54, 50, 54, 51, 55, 53 55, 55, 54, 53, 52, and 53.

Because of the decision to collect the data as discreet whole numbers, these data now have to be analyzed as proportions. With these broad steps there are only five discreet steps within the five-year study period (5 divided by 1), which is below the 10-discrimination-step minimum for variables data. To analyze this data as proportions, for example, we could study the proportion of people 52 years of age or younger or the proportion of people 53 years of age.

The original age data could also have been collected as attributes, where each person in the above group of people was asked if he or she was 53 or older. The collected data would then have looked as follows:

Is Your Age 53 or Older?

Yes	Yes
Yes	Yes
No	Yes
Yes	Yes
No	No
Yes	Yes
No	

These are attribute data, which can only be studied as proportional data. For example, the proportion of yes or no answers could be calculated directly from the data, and then the resultant proportion could be used in an analysis.

What we saw in the above examples is that data collected on an event can often be either variables or proportional, based on the manner in which they are collected and their resolution or discrimination. Attribute data, however, are always treated as proportions (after determining a ratio).

There are some data that are numerical but only available at discreet levels. Shoe size is an example. By definition the steps are discreet, with no information available for values between the shoe sizes. Discreet data are often treated as proportions because the steps may limit the discrimination versus the range of interest.

Let's look at another example, this time using shaft dimensions. Assume that a shaft has a maximum allowable diameter of 1.020 inches and a minimum allowable diameter of 0.080 inch, which is a tolerance of 0.040 inch. Here is the first set of data for shaft diameter in inches:

1.008	1.009
0.982	1.002
0.996	1.003
1.017	0.991
0.997	1.009
1.000	1.014

Since the dimensions are to the third decimal place, these measurement "steps" are small compared to the need (the 0.040-inch tolerance). Since there are 40 discrimination steps (0.040 inch divided by 0.001 inch), these data can be analyzed as variables data.

Suppose, however, that the same shafts diameters were measured as follows:

1.01	1.01
0.98	1.00
1.00	1.00
1.02	0.99
1.00	1.01
1.00	1.01

Since the accuracy of the numbers is now only to two decimal places, the steps within the 0.040-inch tolerance are only four (0.040 inch divided by 0.010 inch), which is below the rule-of-thumb 10-discrimination-step minimum. We must therefore analyze this data as proportions. For example, we could calculate the proportion of shafts that are below 1.00 inch and use that information in an analysis.

Similarly, the same data could have been collected as attributes, checking whether the shafts were below 1.000 inch in diameter, yes or no, determined by a go/no-go gauge set at 1.000 inch. The collected data would then look like the list below:

Is the Shaft Below 1.000 Inch in Diameter?

No	No
Yes	No
Yes	No
No	Yes
Yes	No
No	No

These are attribute data, which can only be analyzed as proportional data. The proportion of yes or no answers can be calculated and then used in an analysis.

Again, what we saw in the above example is that data collected on the same event could be either variables or proportional, based on the manner they were measured and the discrimination. Once you understand this concept, it is quite simple. Since all measurements at some point become stepped due to measurement limitations, these steps must be reasonably small compared to the range of interest if we wish to use the data as variables. Data that do not qualify as variables must be treated as proportions.

COLLECTING SAMPLES

In this section, you learn how to take good samples and get good data. This section also discusses why both averages and variation of data are important and why we often do analysis separately on both.

In later chapters you will see how to calculate minimum sample sizes and how to verify that a gauge is giving data that are sufficient for your needs. Just as important, however, is making sure that your sample and data truly represent the population of the process you wish to measure. The whole intent of sampling is to be able to analyze a process or population and get valid results without measuring every part, so sampling details are extremely important.

Here are some examples of issues in getting good data:

Manufacturing

Samples and the resultant data have to represent the total population, yet processes controlling the population are often changing dramatically, due to people, environment, equipment, and similar factors.

Sales

Sales forecasts often use sampling techniques in their predictions. Yet, the total market may have many diverse groups to sample affected by many external drivers, like the economy.

Marketing

What data should be used to judge a marketing campaign's effectiveness since so many other factors are changing at the same time?

Software Development

What are the main causes of software crashes, and how would you get data to measure the "crash-resistance" of competing software?

Receivables

How would you get good data on the effectiveness of a program intended to reduce overdue receivables, when factors like the economy exert a strong influence and change frequently?

Insurance

How can data measuring customer satisfaction with different insurance programs be compared when the people covered by the programs are not identical?

We have all seen the problems pollsters have in predicting election outcomes based on sampling. In general the problem has not been in the statistical analysis of the data or in the sample size. The problem has been picking a group of people to sample that truly represents the electorate.

The population is not uniform. There are pockets of elderly, wealthy, poor, Democrats, Republicans, urbanites, and suburbanites, each with their own agendas that may affect the way they vote. And, neither the pockets nor their agendas are uniform or static. So, even using indicators from past elections does not guarantee that a pollster's sample will replicate the population as a whole.

The problem of sampling and getting good data has several key components. First, the people and the methods used for taking the samples and data affect the randomness and accuracy of both. Second, the population is diverse and often changing, sometimes quite radically. These changes occur over time and can be affected by location. To truly reflect a population, anyone sampling and using data must be aware of all these variables and somehow get valid data despite them.

The Hawthorne Effect

As soon as anyone goes out to measure a process, things change. Everyone pays more attention. The process operators are more likely to monitor their process and quality inspectors are likely to be more effective in segregating defects. The resultant product you are sampling is not likely to represent that of a random process.

There have been many studies done on how people react to having someone pay attention to them. Perhaps the most famous is the Hawthorne Study, which was done at a large Bell Western manufacturing facility—the Hawthorne Works— in Cicero, Illinois, from 1927 to 1932. This study showed that any gain realized during a controlled test often came from the positive interaction between the people doing the test and the participants, and also from the interaction between the participants. The people may begin to work together as a team to get positive results. The actual change being tested was often not the driver of any improvement.

One of the tests at the Hawthorne facility involved measuring how increasing the light level would influence productivity. The productivity did indeed increase where the light level was increased. But in a control group where the light level was not changed, productivity also improved by the same amount. It was apparently the attention given to both groups by the researchers that was the positive influence, not the light level. In fact, when the light level was restored to its previous level, the productivity remained improved for some time. Thus the effect of attention on research subjects has become known as the Hawthorne effect.

Any data you take that shows an improvement must be suspect due to the Hawthorne effect. Your best protection from making an incorrect assumption about improvement is to take data simultaneously from a parallel line with an identical process (control group), but without the change. However, the people in both groups should have had the same attention, attended the same meetings, and so on. An alternative method is to collect line samples just before and just after the change is implemented, but do so after all the meetings and other interaction have concluded. The before samples would be compared to the after samples, with the assumption that any Hawthorne effect would be included in both.

Other Sampling Difficulties

I once ran a test where product was being inspected online, paced by the conveyor speed. I collected both the rejected product and the packed "good" product from this time period. Without telling the inspectors, I then mixed the defective product with the good packed product and had the same inspectors inspect this remixed product off-line, where the inspectors weren't machine paced. The defect rate almost doubled.

When the product was inspected without time restraints, the quality criteria apparently tightened, even though no one had triggered a change in the criteria. Or maybe the inspectors had just become more effective. Another possibility is that the inspectors felt that I was checking on their effectiveness in finding all the defects, so they were being extra conservative in interpreting the criteria. In any case, someone using data from the off-line inspection would get a defect rate almost double that seen online.

Case Study: Adjusting Data

I was watching a person inspecting product on a high-speed production line. On a regular basis, the inspector picked a random product from the conveyor and placed that product onto a fixture that took key measurements. The measurements from the fixture were displayed on the inspector's computer screen and then automatically sent to the quality database unless the inspector overrode the sending of the data. The override was intended only if the inspector saw a non-product-related problem, like the product not being seated properly in the fixture.

As I was observing, I saw the inspector periodically override the sending of the data even though I saw no apparent problem with the product seating. When I asked the inspector why she was not sending the data, she replied that the readings looked unusual and she didn't feel that they were representative of the majority of product. She didn't want what she thought was erroneous data sent to the system, so she overrode the sending of the data and went to the next product.

She proudly told me that she had been doing that for years and that she had trained other inspectors accordingly. So much for using *those* data! Anyone running a test on this line and then taking his or her own quality samples would likely find more variation in the self-inspected samples than the quality system's historical data would show.

Getting random samples from a conveyor belt is not always easy. Production equipment can have multiple heads that load onto a conveyor belt in a nonrandom fashion. Some of the heads on the production machine may have all of their products sent down one side of the conveyor. The result is that someone taking samples from one side of the conveyor belt will never see product from some of the production heads.

The start-up of any piece of equipment often generates an unusually high incidence of defects. After a shift change, it may take some time for the new operator to get a machine running to his or her own parameters, during which time the quality may suffer. Absenteeism and vacations cause inexperienced people to operate equipment, which in turn generally causes lower quality. Maintenance schedules can often be sensed in product quality. And, of course, there are variables of humidity, temperature, and so on.

Overall quality is a composite of all the above variables and more. In fact, a case could be made that many quality issues come from these "exception" mini-populations. So, how can you possibly sample such that all these variables are taken into account?

First, you probably can't take samples at all the possible combinations listed above. In fact, before you begin to take any samples, you have to go back to the DMAIC process and define the problem. Only with a good definition of the problem will you be able to ascertain what to sample.

AVERAGE AND VARIATION

Before we begin to collect data, we have to understand how we are going to use that data. In Six Sigma we generally are interested in both how the average of the data differs from a nominal target and the variation between the data. What follows is some discussion on how we describe data in Six Sigma terms and why we collect data in the manner we do.

Sigma

One of the ways to describe the measure of the variation of a product is to use the mathematical term *sigma*. We will learn more about sigma and how to calculate this value as we proceed, but for now it is enough to know that the smaller the sigma value, the smaller the amount of process variation; the larger the sigma value, the greater the amount of process variation. In general, you want to minimize sigma (variation).

Ideally the sigma value is very small in comparison to the allowable tolerance on a part or process. If so, the process variation will be small compared with the tolerance a customer requires. When this is the case, the process is "tight" enough that, even if the process is somewhat off-center, the process produces product well within the customer's needs.

Many companies have processes with a relatively large variation compared to their customers' needs (a relatively high sigma value compared to the allowable tolerance). These companies run at an average ±3 sigma level (a three sigma process). This means that 6 sigma (±3 sigma) fit between the tolerance limits. The smaller the sigma, the more sigma that fit within the tolerance, as you can see in Figure 5-1.

Sigma level is calculated by dividing the process allowable tolerance (upper specification minus lower specification) by twice the process sigma value, since the sigma level of a process is stated as a plus-or-minus value. Here is the formula:

$$\text{Process sigma level} = \pm \frac{\text{process tolerance}}{2 \times \text{process sigma value}}$$

As an example, suppose a bearing grinding process has the following measurements:

Sigma = 0.002 inch
Maximum allowable bearing diameter = 1.006 inches

FIGURE 5-1

Two different process sigmas.
From Warren Brussee, *All About Six Sigma.*

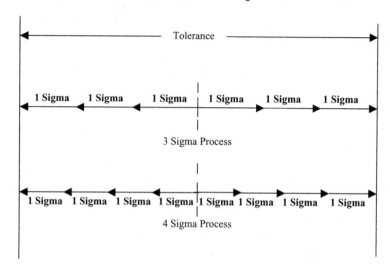

Minimum allowable bearing diameter = 0.994 inches

So the tolerance is 1.006 − 0.994 = 0.012 inch. Putting these values into the above formula:

$$\text{Process sigma level} = \pm \frac{\text{process tolerance}}{2 \times \text{process sigma value}}$$

$$= \pm \frac{0.012 \text{ inch}}{2 \times 0.002 \text{ inch}}$$

$$= \pm 3$$

So this process is running at ±3 sigma, or in the terms of Six Sigma, this is a 3 sigma process.

As you will see in Chapter 7, a 3 sigma process generates 99.73 percent good product, or 997,300 good parts for every 1,000,000 parts produced. This means that there are 2,700 defective products for every 1,000,000 parts produced (or 2,700 input errors per 1,000,000 computer entries, and so on).

Note that some Six Sigma statistics books show the defect level for a 3 sigma process as a radically higher number. If you see a defect level of 66,807 defects per million for a 3 sigma process (versus the 2,700 indicated above), it is because the other book is using Motorola's Six Sigma defect table which includes an assumed 1.5 sigma long-term process drift. The 2,700 defects per million used in this book is consistent with the general statistics tables which will be shown in Chapter 7. In any case, just don't be surprised if some Six Sigma books include the 1.5 sigma drift in their numbers. Including or not including this long-term assumed drift is largely academic as long as you are consistent in your data comparisons.

Since almost all Six Sigma work you will be doing involves data collected and compared over a relatively short period of time (several days or weeks), including an assumed long-term drift will just confuse any analysis and give misleading results. So we don't include an assumed 1.5 sigma drift in this book. Chapter 9 will address how to minimize any long-term process drift.

The defects associated with a 3 sigma process are costly, causing scrap, rework, returns, and lost customers. Eliminating this lost product has the potential to be a profitable "hidden factory" because all the costs and efforts have been expended to produce the product, yet the product is unusable because of quality issues. In today's economic environment, recovering this hidden factory is more important than ever.

Just for interest, a Six Sigma process runs with a variation such that ± 6 sigma (12 sigma), including the Motorola assumed process drift, fit within the tolerance limits. This will generate three defects per million parts produced. This was the original quality goal of this methodology, and it is how the name "Six Sigma" became associated with this process. A three-defects-per-million defect incidence is not required in most real-world situations, and the cost of getting to that quality level is usually not justified. However, getting the quality to a level at which the customer is extremely happy and supplier losses are very low is generally a cost-effective goal, which is important in our current lean times.

It is important to differentiate between the error caused by the average measurement being different than a nominal target and the error caused by variations within the product or process.

No one knows how to make anything perfect. For example, if you were to buy fifty 1.000-inch-diameter bearings and then measure the bearings, you would find that they are not exactly 1.000 inch in diameter. They may be extremely close to 1.000 inch, but if you measure them carefully with a precision device you will find that the bearings are not exactly 1.000 inch.

The bearings will vary from the 1.000-inch nominal diameter in two different ways. First, the average diameter of the 50 bearings will not be exactly 1.000 inch. The amount the average deviates from the target 1.000 inch is due to the bearing manufacturing process being off center.

The second reason that the bearings will differ from the target is that there will be some spread of measurements around the average bearing diameter. This spread of dimensions may be extremely small, but there will be a spread. This is due to the bearing process variation.

If the combination of the off-center bearing process and the bearing process variation is small compared to your needs (tolerance), then you will be satisfied with the bearings. If the combination of the off-center bearing process and the bearing process variation is large compared to your needs, then you will not be satisfied with the bearings. The Six Sigma methodology strives to make the combined effect of an off-center process and process variation small compared to the need (tolerance).

Let's suppose that the bearings you purchased were all larger in diameter than the 1.000-inch nominal diameter. Figure 5-2 illustrates the diameters of these bearings, including the variation. Since the maximum diameter as illustrated is less than the maximum tolerance, these bearings would be acceptable.

FIGURE 5-2

Bearing diameters.
From Warren Brussee, *All About Six Sigma.*

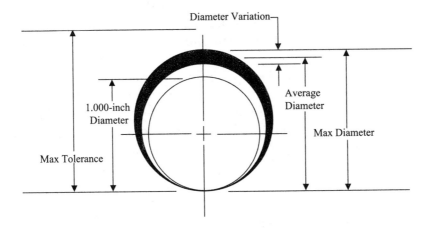

Off-Center Process

You have a dimensional problem on some ground pins. Is the problem that the grinding process is off center and on average they run too large? If a problem is of this nature, it is best addressed by centering the whole process, not focusing on the variation caused by the exception mini-populations. If being off center is the issue, then collecting samples and/ or data and measuring change are a lot easier than if you had to gather samples and/or data on each peculiar part of the population.

When attempting to measure your success on centering a process or changing the process average, you want to collect samples or use data that represent a "normal" process, both before and after any process adjustment. You don't want samples from any of the temporary mini-populations.

One of the ways to identify the normal population is to make a fishbone diagram where the head of the fish is "nonnormal populations." In this way the bones of the fish (the variables) will be all the variables that cause a population to be other than normal. You will then make sure that the time period in which you collect samples and/or data does not have any of the conditions listed on the fishbone.

Let's look at an example. Let's say the problem is the aforementioned issue that ground pins are generally running too large. Let's look at the fishbone diagram for this problem in Figure 5-3.

We can use the key process input variables (KPIVs) shown on this fishbone to determine which ones would likely cause the ground pin diameters to run off center, generally too large. The expert-picked KPIVs are experience of the operator, grinder wheel wear and setup, and gauge verification.

The experience of the operator would perhaps cause this issue for short periods but not as an ongoing problem. At times we would expect to have an experienced operator. Gauge setup and verification could account for the problem since the gauge could be reading off center such that the diameters would be generally too large. However, for this example, let's assume we check and are satisfied that the sim-

FIGURE 5-3

Fishbone diagram—input variables affecting pin diameter errors.
From Warren Brussee, *All About Six Sigma*.

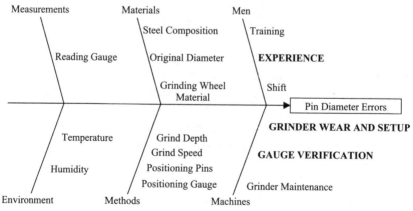

plified gauge verifications (which will be covered in detail in Chapter 6) have been done on schedule and correctly.

That leaves grinding wheel wear and setup. Grinding wheel wear could cause the diameters to change, but then the cycle would start over as the grinding wheel is changed. However, if the grinding wheel setup is incorrect, it could position the grinding wheel incorrectly all the time. This could conceivably cause the diameters to be generally high. So, this is the variable we want to test.

We will want to test having the operator set up the grinding wheel with a different nominal setting to see if this will make the process more on center. We want to do random sampling during the process with the grinding wheel setup being the only variable that we change.

Since the effect of grinding wheel setup is what we want to measure, we want to control all the other input variables. As in the fishbone diagram in Figure 5-3, we especially want experienced people working on the process and want to be sure that the simplified gauge verification was done. These were the input variables that had been defined by the experts as being critical. We will also use a grinding wheel with average wear, so grinding wheel wear is not an issue. The test length for getting samples will be short enough that any additional grinding wheel wear during the test will be negligible.

We will use an experienced crew on day shift, verifying that the pin material is correct and the grinder is set up correctly (grind depth, grind speed, position of pin and gauge). We will make sure grinder maintenance has been done and that the person doing the measurements is experienced. We will minimize the effects of temperature and humidity by taking samples and/or data on the normal process and then immediately performing the test with the revised setup and taking the test samples and/or data. We will only take samples and/or data during these control periods.

Note that we used the fishbone to both show the KPIVs and help pick the input variables we logically concluded could be causing the issue. Without this process of elimination, we would have had to test many more times, wasting time and money. By limiting and controlling our tests, we can concentrate on getting the other variables under control, at least as much as possible.

TIP

Getting good samples and data

Use good problem definition, a fishbone diagram, and any of the other qualitative tools to minimize the number of variables you have to test and then do a good job controlling the other variables during the test. This need to limit required testing is especially important in our current lean environment, because excessive testing can be time-consuming and very expensive.

If this test on grinding wheel setup did not solve the problem of pin diameters being too large, we would then go back and review our logic, perhaps picking another variable to test.

Sample sizes and needed statistical analysis will be covered in Chapter 8. In this chapter we are only emphasizing the non-numerical problems related to getting good data.

Centering or Variation

The above examples showed ways to get good samples and/or data when the problem definition indicated that the problem was related to a process not centered. As you will see later in the book, centering a process, or moving its average, is generally much easier than reducing its variation. Reducing a process variation often involves a complete change in the process, not just a minor adjustment. If the problem definition indicates that the problem is large variation and that the centering of the process is not the issue, then you would have no choice but to try to identify the individual causes of the variation and try to reduce their effect.

Again, you will save yourself a lot of trouble if you can make the problem definition more specific than just stating that the variation is too high. Does the problem happen on a regular or spaced frequency? Is it related to shift, machine, product, operator, or day? Any specific information will dramatically reduce the number of different mini-populations from which you will have to gather samples and/or data. This more specific problem definition will then be compared to the related fishbone diagram to try to isolate the conditions that you must sample.

Process with Too Much Variation

Suppose our earlier ground-pin-diameter error had been defined as being periodic, affecting one machine at a time and not being a process off-center problem. Figure 5-4 shows the fishbone diagram with this new problem definition in mind.

Since the problem is defined as periodic, let's see which of these input variables would likely have a production line time period associated with the problem. It appears that each KPIV (experience, grinding wheel wear and setup, gauge

FIGURE 5–4

Fishbone diagram—input variables affecting pin diameter errors.
From Warren Brussee, *All About Six Sigma*.

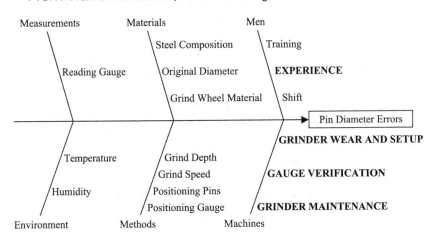

verification, and grinder maintenance) may have different time periods. With this insight, we can go back and see if it is possible to get an even better problem definition that will allow us to focus more sharply on the specific problem.

Assume that we go back to the customer or whoever triggered the issue and find that the problem occurs every several weeks on each line but not on all lines at the same time. Let's look at our KPIVs with this in mind. Experience would be random, not every several weeks. The grinding wheels are replaced every several days, so the time period doesn't match. Simplified gauge verifications are done monthly, so that cycle also doesn't fit. However, grinder maintenance is done on a two-week cycle, one machine at a time. This variable fits the problem definition. We now need to run a controlled test.

We want to control everything other than grinder maintenance during our sample and/or data collection. We will change the grinding wheel frequently, verifying its setup to make sure that is not an issue. We will have experienced people working on the process, and we will be sure that simplified gauge verification was done. All of these input variables have been defined by the experts as being critical, so we want to be sure to have them in control.

We will use an experienced crew on day shift, verifying that the pin and grinding wheel materials are correct, the grinder is set up correctly (grinder depth and/or speed, position of pin and gauge), and that an experienced person will be doing the measurements. We will minimize the effects of temperature and humidity by taking samples and/or data at the same time each day. Since we don't know if the problem is caused by not doing grinder maintenance often enough or if the grinder takes some time to debug after maintenance, we probably want to take samples daily for at least two weeks to get a better idea of the actual cause.

As you can see in all the above examples, good problem definition combined with a fishbone diagram will focus us on what samples and/or data we need. The detail within the fishbone will further help us make sure that the other variables in the process being measured are as stable as possible, with the exception of the variable being evaluated.

Once a change is implemented, samples and/or data must be collected to verify that the improvement actually happened.

WHAT WE HAVE LEARNED IN CHAPTER 5

- All the statistics that we do in Six Sigma use only two types of data: variables and proportional.
- Variables data are normally measurements expressed as decimals. This data can theoretically be measured to whatever degree of accuracy desired, which is why they are sometimes called continuous data. On variables data, the measurement resolution should be sufficient to give at least 10 steps within the range of interest.
- Proportional data are always ratios or probabilities. Proportional data are often expressed as decimals, but these decimals are ratios rather than from actual physical measurements. Any data that doesn't qualify as variables must be treated as proportions.
- Getting valid samples and data is just as important as the application of any statistical tool.
- Use the fishbone diagram to identify the key process input variables that cause mini-populations. Use the problem definition and close analysis of the fishbone diagram to limit your focus.
- Generally, the easiest approach to improving a process output quality is to center the total process rather than reduce the process variation.

CHAPTER 6

Simplified Gauge Verification

In this chapter you learn how to determine gauge error and how to correct this error if excessive. When a problem surfaces, one of the first things that has to be done is to get good data or measurements. The issue of gauge accuracy, repeatability, and reproducibility applies everywhere a variables data measurement (decimals) is taken. Simplified gauge verification is needed to make sure that gauge error is not excessive. The measuring device can be as simple as a micrometer or as complex as a radiation sensor.

Data error can give us a false sense of security—we believe that the process is in control and that we are making acceptable product—or cause us to make erroneous changes to a process. These errors can be compounded by differences between the gauges used by the supplier and those used by the customer, or by variation among gauges within a manufacturing plant. These types of errors can be very costly and must be minimized in our current tight economy.

Earlier in the book we stated that Six Sigma was concerned with how a product or process differed from the nominal case; that any error was due to a combination of the average product being off center plus any variation of the products around that average. A gauge used to measure a product can have similar issues.

For any product of a known dimension, all of the individuals measuring that product with a particular gauge will get an error, albeit small. That error will be a combination of the average reading being different than the actual product dimension and a range of measurements around the average reading. Figure 6-1 is a visual representation of a possible set of readings taken on one part. In this case the readings all happen to be greater than the true part dimension.

Figure 6-1 shows the range of actual gauge readings. *Gauge error* is defined as the maximum expected difference among the various gauge readings versus a nominal part's true dimension. In Six Sigma projects, the use of the simplified gauge verification tool often gives insight that allows for big gains with no additional efforts. In the DMAIC process, this tool can be used in the Define, Measure, Analyze, Improve, and Control steps.

> **TIP**
> The maximum allowable gauge error is 30 percent of the tolerance.
>
> Ideally a gauge should not use up more than 10 percent of the tolerance. The maximum allowable gauge error generally used is 30 percent.

FIGURE 6−1

Gauge readings on a product of a known dimension. From Warren Brussee, *All About Six Sigma*.

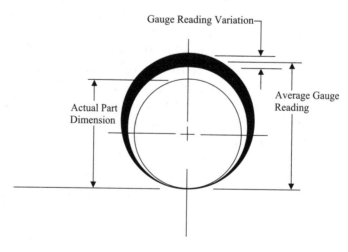

Some plants discover that as many as half of their gauges will not pass the 30 percent maximum error criteria. Even after extensive rework, many gauges cannot pass the simplified gauge verification because the part tolerance is too tight for the gauge design. Since most plants do not want to run with reduced in-house tolerances, a problem gauge must be upgraded to "use up" less of the tolerance.

CHECKING FOR GAUGE ERROR

In a lean environment, where we want all our efforts to bear the most fruit at the lowest possible cost, checking for gauge error certainly should have high priority. Reducing gauge error can open up a supplier's process window and perhaps enable them to make an acceptable part at a much lower cost.

There are several methods of checking for gauge error. The method discussed in this text emphasizes improving the gauge (when required) rather than retraining inspectors. Inspectors change frequently, and it is nearly impossible to get someone to routinely follow a very detailed and delicate procedure to get a gauge reading accurately. It is better to have a robust gauge that is not likely to be used incorrectly.

Simplified gauge verification includes both repeatability/reproducibility and accuracy. In simple terms, it checks for both the variations in gauge readings and for the correctness of the average gauge reading.

DEFINITIONS

Repeatability/Reproducibility   These terms relate to consistencies in readings from a gauge. Repeatability is the consistency of an individual's gauge readings, and reproducibility is the consistency of multiple people's readings from that same gauge. Simplified gauge verification combines the two.

Accuracy   The term *accuracy* relates to the correctness of the average of all the above readings versus some agreed-upon true measurement value.

TIP

Generate masters for simplified gauge verification

Simplified gauge verification requires several "master" products near the product's specification center. The supplier and customer must agree on the dimensions of these masters.

Masters can be quantified using outside firms that have calibrated specialized measuring devices or by getting mutual agreement between the supplier and customer.

Figure 6-2 gives a visual representation of simplified gauge verification.

The reason the gauge error includes plus or minus the accuracy plus the repeatability/reproducibility is that the tolerance, which is the reference, also includes any allowable plus-or-minus variation on both sides of the process center. This makes the ratio comparison with the tolerance valid.

INSTRUCTIONS FOR SIMPLIFIED GAUGE VERIFICATION

Using a randomly picked master, have three different inspectors (or operators) measure the master seven times each. Have

FIGURE 6-2

Simplified gauge verification.
From Warren Brussee, *All About Six Sigma*.

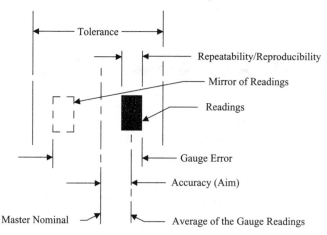

them measure the product as they would in normal production (amount of time, method, and so on). Calculate the average $\bar{x}$ and standard deviation s of *all* 21 readings. If the standard deviation s is calculated on a manual calculator, use the $n-1$ option if available.

FORMULA

Simplified gauge verification, variables data

$$\text{Percent gauge error} = \frac{5s + 2* \left|\text{master} - \bar{x}\right|}{\text{tolerance}} * 100 \text{ percent}$$

Ideally <10 percent; max 30 percent

$\bar{x}$ = average of *all* 21 readings of a master product

s = standard deviation of *all* 21 readings of a master product

Master = standardized dimension of the master product

Tolerance = allowable product tolerance (maximum − minimum)

$\left|\text{Master} - \bar{x}\right|$ = accuracy or aim, ignoring minus signs

---

The reason the s is multiplied by 5 in the formula is that ± 2.5 sigma represents 99 percent of the items on a normal distribution. This means that the formula is indicative of the maximum error that would be expected on 99 percent of the products.

If two times the accuracy $\left|\text{master} - \bar{x}\right|$ is the predominant error (compared to the total gauge error), you should examine the setup procedure for the gauge, specifically the nominal setting. It is normally easier to reduce gauge accuracy error than repeatability/reproducibility error.

We chose to use a master that was close to the center of the specification, which is sufficient in most cases. However, for some types of optical gauges you need to verify readings at both the center and at an end of the specification because mechanical movement of the optics can cause them to read correctly at the center but not at the end. In most cases, however, masters at the center are sufficient.

TIP
Document simplified gauge verification.

Gauge verification must be set up as a regular routine, with documentation kept.

EXAMPLE OF SIMPLIFIED GAUGE VERIFICATION ON BEARINGS

We want to perform the simplified gauge verification procedure to test the gauge we are using to measure the diameters on bearings. We have established a master bearing, which is near nominal. We will now have three inspectors (or operators) measure this master bearing seven times each. Here are the results:

Master bearing standardized reading = 1.0004
Allowable bearing dimensions: Max = 1.0050, min = 0.9960, so tolerance = 0.0090 (all dimensions in inches)

Inspector	Reading Number	Dimension (inches)
A	1	1.0018
	2	1.0001
	3	0.9998
	4	1.0011
	5	0.9996
	6	1.0001
	7	1.0001
B	1	0.9992
	2	1.0011
	3	1.0002
	4	0.9991
	5	1.0004
	6	0.9988
	7	1.001
C	1	0.9997
	2	0.9988
	3	1.0008
	4	1.0015
	5	0.9998
	6	1.0006
	7	0.9996

Average $\bar{x}$ = 1.000152 inches

Standard deviation s = 0.000851 inch

$5s$ = 0.004253 inch

$$\text{Percent gauge error} = \frac{5s + 2 * |\text{master} - \bar{x}|}{\text{tolerance}} * 100 \text{ percent}$$

$$= \frac{0.0043 + 2 * |1.0004 - 1.0002|}{0.0090} * 100 \text{ percent}$$

$$= 52 \text{ percent}$$

Since the calculated gauge error of 52 percent exceeds the allowable 30 percent, we must go back and rework or recalibrate the gauge. Assume we rework the gauge. Here are the gauge readings after rework:

Master bearing standardized reading = 1.0004
Allowable bearing dimensions: Max = 1.0050, min = 0.9960, so tolerance = 0.0090 (all dimensions in inches)

Inspector	Reading Number	Dimension (inches)
A	1	1.0008
	2	1.0006
	3	1.0001
	4	1.0011
	5	1.0004
	6	0.9998
	7	1.0007
B	1	0.9996
	2	0.9999
	3	1.001
	4	1.0005
	5	1.0001
	6	1.0003
	7	1.0002
C	1	1.0007
	2	1.0006
	3	0.9996
	4	0.9999
	5	1.0004
	6	1.0006
	7	1.0003

Average $\bar{x} = 1.000343$
Standard deviation $s = 0.000426$
$5s = 0.002131$

$$\text{Percent gauge error} = \frac{5s + 2*\left|\text{master} - \bar{x}\right|}{\text{tolerance}} *100 \text{ percent}$$

$$= \frac{0.0021 + 0.0001}{0.0090} *100 \text{ percent}$$

$$= 24.4 \text{ percent}$$

Although the calculated gauge error of 24.4 percent is not great, it is acceptable. Note that by just looking at the raw readings before and after rework, it is not obvious whether the gauge is doing an acceptable job, even when reading a master bearing with a known diameter. That is why simplified gauge verification often yields a great payback; it is a hidden problem (opportunity).

TIP
Take advantage of simplified gauge verification.

If you have gauges that take critical measurements and simplified gauge verification has not been done, you have a real opportunity to make a substantial improvement. This is especially true if the customer has reported any problems related to the product or if quality losses are high.

GAUGE R&R

Most Six Sigma classes and books teach a process called *gauge R&R* to check gauges. Gauge R&R only addresses repeatability and reproducibility, not accuracy (aim). Gauge R&R uses current production products, rather than masters. To get valid gauge R&R test results, the current production products must include the full range of process dimensions, which are not always readily available. If the test samples do not include the full range of process dimensions, the gauge R&R will often not pass.

Simplified gauge verification combines repeatability/reproducibility and accuracy into one test and emphasizes total gauge error. If there is an ongoing issue with a gauge, the gauge must be redesigned for ease of use so operator error is minor and included as part of the total gauge error. This approach is based on much experience (frustration) on the difficulty of getting a changing group of inspectors to follow precise instructions on taking measurements.

WHAT WE HAVE LEARNED IN CHAPTER 6

- In the DMAIC process, simplified gauge verification can be used in the Define, Measure, Analyze, Improve, and Control steps.
- Ideally a gauge should not use up more than 10 percent of the allowable tolerance. The maximum allowed is generally 30 percent.
- The first step in simplified gauge verification is to get one or more master products near the specification center. The supplier and customer must agree on the dimensions of these masters.
- Emphasize improving the gauge (when required) rather than retraining inspectors.
- The simplified gauge verification formula includes both repeatability/reproducibility (ability to duplicate a reading) and accuracy (aim, or correctness of average reading).

PART FOUR

Probability, Plots, and Statistical Tests

Data Overview

PROBABILITY

In this chapter you learn to let data drive problem solving. However, to interpret data you need to make a judgment as to whether unusual results were due to random cause—for example, someone is flipping a coin and getting an excessive number of heads by chance—or due to an assignable cause—for example, someone is flipping a coin that has two heads. Knowledge of probability assists you in making this determination with a minimum number of samples (coin flips in this example). Here are some examples of how probability is established:

Manufacturing

On any production line with multiple heads, compare defect levels from each head to see if they are significantly different. Compare production lines, shifts, defects on different days of the week, and so on.

Sales

Compare salespeople. The criteria could include new customers, sales, etc. Cross training between the best and worst performers can often improve both.

Marketing

Check if sales increased significantly after a marketing campaign.

Accounting and Software Development

Compare error incidence for significant difference between groups.

Receivables

Check the effect of increased or decreased monitoring of overdue receivables.

Insurance

Compare the complaints at different treatment centers. The criteria could include patient care and billing errors.

Often data you want to analyze will have some related probability that can assist. For example, if you have a manufactured part with four sides and a defect is always on one of the sides, understanding probability could help you find the defect cause. If there are eight salespeople, but one salesperson is generating 25 percent of the total sales, you may want to get the other salespeople to emulate the best salesperson. However, you first have to be sure that the results are not due to just random chance but instead are truly indicative of a real difference.

Uses of Probability

In the course of our daily lives, we frequently make estimates on the likelihood of an event or its probability. Examples are the chance of rain, winning the lottery, or being in a plane crash. Some probabilities are easy to calculate and intuit: for example, figuring the chance of getting a head on a coin flip (1 in 2, or 0.5). Some probabilities are not easy to calculate or intuit, like the probability of an earthquake.

In Six Sigma we also need to make an estimate of the probability of an event. In this way we can make some judgment as to whether something happened due to random coincidence or due to an assignable cause that we should address.

We will start with problems where we know the mathematical probability of a single random event and use Excel's BINOMDIST to get an answer.

DEFINITIONS

n   This variable represents the number of independent trials, like the number of coin tosses or the number of parts measured.

Probability *p* (or probability *s*)   This is the probability of a success on each individual trial, like the likelihood of a head on one coin flip or a defect on one part. This is always a proportion and generally shown as a decimal, like 0.0156.

Number *s* (or *x* successes)   This is the total number of successes that you are looking for, like getting exactly three heads.

Probability *P*   This is the probability of getting a given number of successes from all the trials, like the probability of three heads in five coin tosses or 14 defects in a shipment of 1,000 parts. This is often the answer to the problem.

Cumulative   This is the sum of the probabilities of getting the number of successes or less, like getting three or less heads on five flips of a coin. This option is used on less-than and more-than problems.

These definitions and their uses will become apparent as you solve the following problems.

PROBLEM 1

What are the chances of getting exactly two heads in three flips of a coin?

We will solve this using Excel. After bringing up the Excel worksheet, click on *fx* (Paste function or Insert function) in the toolbar. Under Category, click on Statistical. Then, under Function, click on BINOMDIST.

In the first box, enter the number of successes (number of heads) you want in these trials, which is 2. The second box asks for the number of trials, which is 3. The third box asks for the probability of a success (head) on each trial, which is 0.5.

The fourth box asks if the problem requires the cumulative probability. If you answer True, you get the sum of the probabilities up to and including 2 (the probability of zero heads plus the probability of 1 head plus the probability of 2 heads), which is the probability of getting 2 or less heads. In this problem you do *not* want the cumulative probability, so answer False. You then get our desired probability of exactly 2 heads, which is $P = 0.375$.

Here is a summary of what we just did:

Excel BINOMDIST
Number of successes = 2
Trials = 3
Probability = 0.5
Cumulative: false
The result is $P = 0.375$.

TIP
Use the sum of probabilities = 1.

Since the sum of the probabilities of all possible outcomes always equals 1, we can often use this knowledge to simplify a problem.

For example, if we want to know the probability of getting 1 or more heads on 10 coin tosses, we can find the probability of getting zero heads then subtract this probability from 1. This is much easier than adding the probabilities of 1 head + 2 heads + 3 heads + 4 heads + 5 heads + 6 heads + 7 heads + 8 heads + 9 heads + 10 heads.

PROBLEM 2

What is the probability of getting two or less heads in three flips of a coin?

We show three ways to solve this problem:

Using the BINOMDIST in Excel, you can do it three times, adding the results of zero, 1, and 2 successes (with cumulative false) and you get 0.125 + 0.375 + 0.375 = 0.875.

Or you can recognize that the only outcome that has more than 2 heads is 3 heads. Using Excel's BINOMDIST, we find that the probability of 3 heads is 0.125. Since the sum of the probabilities of all possible outcomes always equals 1, we can subtract the probability of 3 heads (0.125) from 1 to get the answer 0.875.

The following is the most direct way to the answer. Using Excel BINOMDIST, we can realize that the cumulative true gives the probability of getting 2 or less heads, which is what we want. So, here's how we can get the answer directly:

Excel BINOMDIST
Number of successes = 2
Trials = 3
$p = 0.5$
Cumulative: true
The result is $P = 0.875$.

TIP
Using Excels BINOMDIST cumulative function

Don't use the cumulative function for the probability of a single outcome/success, like 3 heads out of 5 coin tosses. Enter False in the box for cumulative function.

Use the cumulative function for Less than, Equal to or less than, Equal to or more than, or More than a given outcome or success, as follows.

For less than a given outcome, like less than 3 heads out of 8 coin tosses, use the cumulative function True with the success at 1 less than the given value $(3 - 1 = 2)$.

Success = 2
Trials = 8
$p = 0.5$
Cumulative: true
The result is $P = 0.1445$

For equal to or less than a given outcome, like 3 heads or less out of 8 coin tosses, use the cumulative function True with the success at the given value (3).

Success = 3
Trials = 8
$p = 0.5$
Cumulative: true
The result is $P = 0.3633$

For more than a given outcome, like more than 3 heads out of 8 coin tosses, use the cumulative function True with the success at the given value (3), then subtract the result from 1.

Success = 3
Trials = 8
$p = 0.5$
Cumulative: true
The result is 0.3633. P would then equal $1.0000 - 0.3633 = 0.6367$.

For equal to or more than a given outcome, like 3 or more heads out of 8 coin tosses, use the cumulative function True with the success at 1 less than the given outcome $(3 - 1 = 2)$, then subtract the result from 1.

Success = 2
Trials = 8
$p = 0.5$
Cumulative: true
The result is 0.1445. P would then equal $1.0000 - 0.1445 = 0.8555$.

PROBLEM 3

What is the chance of getting 7 or less tails on 10 flips of a coin?

Excel BINOMDIST
Successes = 7
Trials = 10
$p = 0.5$
Cumulative: true
The result is $P = 0.9453$

TIP
Independent trials are not affected by earlier results.

The probability on an independent trial is *not* affected by results on earlier trials. For example, someone could have flipped 10 heads in a row, but the probability of a head on the next coin flip is still $p = 0.5$ assuming both the coin and the person tossing it are honest, and so on.

PROBLEM 4

What are the chances of getting at least 7 tails on 10 coin flips?
Using the Excel BINOMDIST and realizing that the chance of at least 7 tails (or 7 or more tails) is the same as 1 minus the chance of 6 or less tails, we solve as follows:

Excel BINOMDIST
Successes = 6
Trials = 10
$p = 0.5$
Cumulative: true
The result is 0.8281. P would then equal $1.0000 - 0.8281 = 0.1719$, or 17.19 percent.

PROBLEM 5

A vendor is making 12.5 percent defective product. In a box of 10 random parts from this vendor, what is the probability of finding 2 or less defects?

Excel BINOMDIST
Success = 2
Trials = 10
$p = 0.125$
Cumulative: true
The result is $P = 0.880$, or 88.0 percent.

PROBLEM 6

A salesperson has been losing 30 percent of potential sales. In a study of 10 random sales contacts from this salesperson, what is the probability of finding 3 or more successful sales?

We must be careful that what we call a "success" (*successful* sales in this case) is consistent with the rest of the problem statement (which is currently stated as the percentage of *lost* sales). We can restate the question as "getting 70 percent of potential sales" so the success is measured in the same terms as the rest of the problem statement. Then we have the following problem.

A salesperson has been successful in getting 70 percent of potential sales. In a study of 10 random sales contacts from this salesperson, what is the probability of finding 3 or more successful sales?

Again, to save work, we know that "3 or more successful sales" is the same as 1 minus the probability of "2 or less successful sales":

Excel BINOMDIST

Success = 2

Trials = 10

$p = 0.70$

Cumulative: true

The result is 0.0016. P would then equal $1.0000 - 0.0016 = 0.9984$, or 99.84 percent.

Case Study: Most Defects from One Machine

A product had a hole stamped by one of two machines. These machines also stamped an identification mark on the product so that someone could identify which machine stamped the hole. A quality engineer randomly collected 80 parts with defective holes. He examined them and found that 49 defects were from one of the two machines. He concluded that there was less than a 3 percent chance that 49 or more defects out of 80 would be coming from one machine due to random cause alone.

So he went looking for anything suspect on the machine that was making most of the defects. He found that the fixture that held the product on the machine had a burr on one side, causing the product to be slightly out of line while the hole was being punched. He had the machine operator remove the burr and the product then seated properly.

The engineer then rechecked another random 80 defective holes and this time found no significant difference between the two machines.

Let's see if we agree with the engineer's conclusion that the higher number of defects coming from one machine was probably not due to random cause alone. Note that he checked the chances of 49 *or more* defects happening randomly, since there was nothing special about being *exactly* 49.

Excel BINOMDIST

Successes = 48

Trials =80

$p = 0.5$ (1/2, the probability of the defect randomly coming from one machine)

Cumulative: true

The result is 0.9717. P would then equal 1.0000 − 0.9717 = 0.0283, or 2.83 percent.

So, there is only a 2.83 percent chance of getting 49 or more of the 80 defects from one machine due to random results. So the engineer was right to be suspicious—and his conclusion enabled him to focus his attention on the one machine, which minimized the areas he had to examine to identify the problem source.

MAXIMUM 1,000 TRIALS IN EXCEL BINOMDIST

Excel BINOMDIST allows a maximum of 1,000 trials. So, if you have more than 1,000 trials, proportion the trials and number of successes to 1,000.

For example, if the data consist of 2,000 trials and you are looking for 140 successes, use Excel BINOMDIST with 1,000 trials and 70 successes. The p is not affected.

PROBLEM 7

These are the results of 109 random erroneous orders processed by seven telephone operators, A through G:

A 14	E 16
B 15	F 15
C 23	G 13
D 13	

Is Operator C's performance worse than we should expect, since C's 23-error total is higher than that of the other six operators? We would want to be at least 95 percent confident that the performance was poor before any action was taken.

We want to check against the likelihood of getting 23 *or more* errors, rather than exactly 23. This will be more conservative, and it's not important that there were *exactly* 23 order errors.

Excel BINOMDIST

Successes = 22

Trials = 109

$p = 1/7 = 0.14286$ (random chance since there are seven operators)

Cumulative: true

The result is 0.9662. P would then equal 1.0000 − 0.9662 = 0.0338, or 3.38 percent.

This means that there is a 3.4 percent chance of this happening randomly without an assignable cause. The confidence level of the conclusion that this is not random would therefore be 100 − 3.4 = 96.6 percent, which is greater than the 95 percent test threshold.

Therefore, we can conclude with a 95 percent confidence that Operator C is performing worse than what would be expected. Of course, the reason for the poorer performance could be something as simple as the operator being new on the job.

Note that when checking for significant differences when you have a large number of possibilities (there are seven operators in the above group); the odds increase that at least one will be significantly different than the others. That is not unlike comparing two operators multiple times. If you do enough comparisons you will eventually get a sample that shows significant difference. That is why you never want to overreact to the outcome of one sample, especially if the other variables are not being controlled.

DATA PLOTS AND DISTRIBUTIONS

In this section you learn to plot data and to spot opportunities from these plots. You will also learn what a "normal" distribution of data is and some terminology to describe this distribution. This knowledge, which is required in Six Sigma, will help you solve many real problems. It is used in all steps of the DMAIC methodology. Here are some examples of the use of charts (histograms) and the normal distribution:

Manufacturing

Make histograms on processes, plants, and/or shifts that are supposed to be the same and you may find differences.

Sales

Use histogram charts to compare sales results year to year, by month, or by sales office. You can also compare success in getting new customers or graph additional sales generated per travel dollar.

Marketing

Look at market segments per month and compare changes year to year with marketing campaigns or dollars spent on advertising.

Accounting and Software Development

Use histogram charts to graphically compare employees versus lines of code written or accounting forms completed.

Receivables

Plot the monthly receivables year over year and then compare that graph to the cash flow graph.

Insurance

Compare surgeries done in comparable hospitals to spot cost differences.

In the following paragraphs, I will be introducing some statistical terms that may be unfamiliar to some readers, such as *histogram, normal data*, and *normal distribution*. However, as you read through the related sections, their definitions and uses will become clear. So don't get intimidated by the unfamiliar terms.

Normal Data

A lathe is machining shafts to a 1.0000-inch nominal diameter. You carefully measure 100 diameters of these shafts. If you sort the diameters into 0.0005-inch-wide "bins" and plot these data, you will get a histogram similar to that shown in Figure 7-1. In this illustration, the ends of the shafts are shown for clarity. This would not be shown in a regular histogram.

> **TIP**
> In a histogram assume no values are on bin "edges."
>
> When a value appears to be exactly on a bin "edge," convention is to put that value into the higher bin. In Figure 7-1, if a shaft were measured to be exactly 1.0000 inch, it would be put into the 1.0000- to 1.0005-inch bin.
>
> Not having a value on a bin edge is not difficult to accept when you consider that with an accurate enough measurement system you would be able to see even the smallest difference from exactly 1.0000 inch.

We will now interpret the data in Figure 7-1.

First, notice that the process is centered and that the left half is a mirror image of the right. What percent of the shafts are within 0.001 inch of the 1.000-inch nominal diameter? Adding the bin quantities on both sides of the center ±0.001 inch, we get 68, or 68 percent of the shafts. It will be shown later that on any process with a normal distribution, this 0.68 point (or 0.34 on either side of the center) is equal to ±1 sigma (or ±1 standard deviation).

For illustration purposes, 1 sigma in this case just happens to equal 0.001 inch. Therefore, 2 sigma = 0.002 inch. What percentage of the shafts is within ±2 sigma of the nominal diameter? Again, counting the bin quantities within ±0.002 inch on

FIGURE 7-1

A histogram of 100 shafts, 1-inch nominal shapes sorted into 0.0005-inch-wide bins.
From Warren Brussee, *All About Six Sigma*.

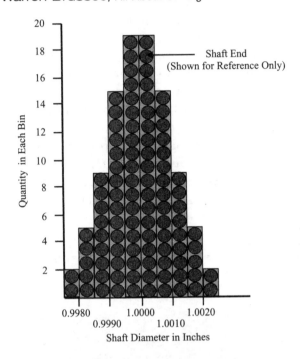

Shaft Diameter in Inches

TIP

Reference data within a normal distribution

It is handy to remember that approximately 2/3 (68 percent) of the data points are within ±1 sigma of the center in a process with a normal distribution and that 95 percent are within ±2 sigma. Another good reference number is that 99.7 percent of the data points are within ±3 sigma of the center.

---

both sides of the center, we find that 96 shafts, or 96 percent of the shafts, are within 2 sigma of the nominal diameter.

All of the preceding questions referred to data on both sides of the center. However, it is often important to know what is occurring on only one end of the data. For example, what percent of the shafts are at least 1 sigma greater than

1.0000-inch diameter? Adding the bin quantities to the right of +1 sigma (sigma in this case happens to be +0.0010 inch), we get 16, or 16 percent.

We will be using charts (and computer programs) that take the reference points at either the center or at either end of the data. You have to look carefully at the data and chart illustration to see what reference point is being used.

Now, using some of the techniques from the previous section on probability and assuming independence (assume you put the first shaft back before picking the second), what is the likelihood of randomly picking two shafts that are above 1.0000 inch in diameter? Since the probability of each is 0.5, the probability of 2 in a row is 0.5 × 0.5 = 0.25.

The preceding example used shafts, but other items could have been plotted with similar results. The height of 16-year-

FIGURE 7-2

Histogram of 1,000 shafts, 1-inch nominal shafts sorted into 0.0001-inch-wide bins.
From Warren Brussee, *All About Six Sigma*.

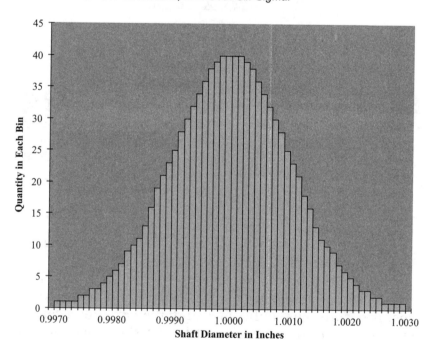

old boys could have been plotted, with the bins representing 1-inch height increments. Points scored by a basketball team could be shown as a histogram, with each bin representing 5 points. Clerical errors could be displayed, with each bin being an increment of errors per 10,000 entries. In all the above cases, you will probably get a normal distribution.

Let's now plot the same population of shaft data using 1,000 shafts and breaking the data into 0.0001-inch-wide bins, as shown in Figure 7-2.

As we get more data from this process and use smaller bins, the shape of the histogram approaches a normal distribution. In fact it helps to think of a normal "curve" as a normal distribution with very small bins. This is the shape that will occur on many processes. Note that ± 1 sigma is at the inflection point on the curve, where the curve changes from convex in the middle to concave at both ends.

Figure 7-3 shows how a normal distribution curve varies with different values of sigma.

FIGURE 7-3

Normal distributions with various sigma values.
From Warren Brussee, *All About Six Sigma*.

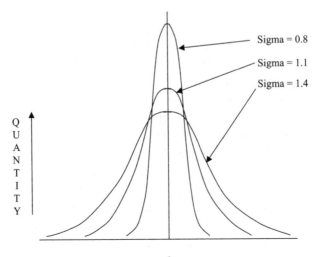

TIP

Specifying a normal distribution

All that is needed to define a normal distributed set of data is the mean (average) and the standard deviation (sigma).

We could calculate the standard deviation (sigma) values manually; but since most $10 calculators and many computer programs do this so easily, we will not manually calculate them. If you use a calculator to calculate sigma and you have your choice of using n or $(n–1)$, use $(n–1)$.

Just for reference, here's the formula to solve for the standard deviation s on a set of n values, where $\overline{x}$ is the average of all the data points x:

$$s = \sqrt{\frac{(x_1 - \overline{x})^2 + (x_2 - \overline{x})^2 + ...(x_n - \overline{x})^2}{n-1}}$$

The standard deviation is a measure of the spread of the normal curve. The greater the sigma, the more distributed the data, with more highs and lows.

The use of normal curve standardized data allows us to make predictions on processes with normal distributions using small samples rather than collecting a large number of data points. As you will see later, once we establish that a process has a normal distribution, we can assume that this distribution will stay normal unless a major process change occurs.

We will be doing a lot of analyses based on the likelihood of randomly finding data beyond ±2 sigma or outside of the expected 95 percent of the data. The case of our 1,000 shafts is depicted in the histogram shown in Figure 7-4 with this 5 percent area darkly shaded on the two ends below 0.9980 inch and above 1.0020 inch.

Figure 7-5 shows how this kind of distribution would look if it were distributed randomly. The figure shows several hundred shafts with 5 percent of the shafts shaded.

If you randomly picked a shaft from the distribution in Figure 7-5, you would be unlikely to pick a shaded one. In fact, if you picked a shaded shaft very often, you would prob-

FIGURE 7−4

Histogram of 1,000 shafts with 5 percent shaded, 1-inch nominal shafts sorted into 0.0001-inch-wide bins. From Warren Brussee, *All About Six Sigma*.

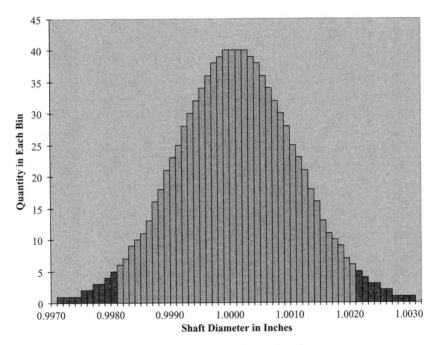

ably begin to wonder if the distribution really had only 5 percent shaded shafts. Much of the analysis we will be doing has similar logic.

Z Value

The standardized normal distribution table in Figure 7-6 is one source of probability values to use on any normal process or set of data. The Z in the table refers to the number of sigma to the right of the center. The probabilities refer to the area to the right of the Z point.

Be aware that some tables (and computer programs) use different reference points, so examine tables and computer programs carefully before using. Satisfy yourself that you

FIGURE 7—5

Random shafts with 5 percent shaded.
From Warren Brussee, *All About Six Sigma*.

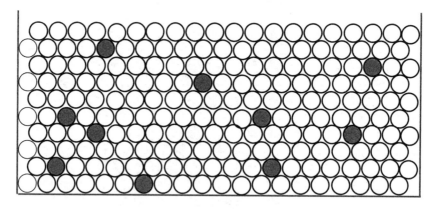

can find data points on the standardized normal distribution table (Figure 7-6) relating to the previous shaft histogram with 0.0001-inch-wide bins (Figure 7-2).

So there is no confusion reading this table, let's be sure that it agrees with our reference number of 2/3 (68 percent) of data points being within ±1 sigma. Looking at the table, with a $Z = 1.00$ (which means a sigma of 1), we get $P = 0.1587$, or approximately 0.16. This is illustrated in Figure 7-7. The left side is a mirror image of the right, as shown in Figure 7-8.

Given that the area under the curve always equals 1 (the sum of all the probabilities equals 1), we know that the white area under the curve = 1 minus the shaded tails. This is 1 − (16 percent + 16 percent) = 1 − 32 percent = 68 percent. This confirms our reference number of 68 percent (or 2/3, which is easy to remember).

PROBLEM 8

In the shaft process previously discussed, what is the probability of finding a shaft at least 2 sigma (0.0020 inch) over

FIGURE 7-6

Standardized normal distribution table.
From Warren Brussee, *All About Six Sigma.*

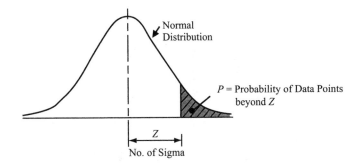

Z	P	Z	P	Z	P	Z	P
0.00	**0.5000**	0.05	0.4801	0.10	0.4602	0.15	0.4404
0.20	0.4207	0.25	0.4013	0.30	0.3821	0.35	0.3632
0.40	0.3446	0.45	0.3264	0.50	0.3085	0.55	0.2912
0.60	0.2743	0.65	0.2578	0.70	0.2420	0.75	0.2266
0.80	0.2119	0.85	0.1977	0.90	0.1841	0.95	0.1711
1.00	**0.1587**	1.05	0.1469	1.10	0.1357	1.15	0.1251
1.20	0.1151	1.25	0.1056	1.30	0.09680	1.35	0.08851
1.40	0.08076	1.45	0.07353	1.50	0.06681	1.55	0.06057
1.60	0.05480	1.65	0.04947	1.70	0.04457	1.75	0.04006
1.80	0.03593	1.85	0.03216	1.90	0.02872	1.95	0.02559
2.00	**0.02275**	2.05	0.02018	2.10	0.01786	2.15	0.01578
2.20	0.01390	2.25	0.01222	2.30	0.01072	2.35	0.009387
2.40	0.008198	2.45	0.007143	2.50	0.006210	2.55	0.005386
2.60	0.004661	2.65	0.004025	2.70	0.003467	2.75	0.002980
2.80	0.002555	2.85	0.002186	2.90	0.001866	2.95	0.001589
3.00	**0.001350**	3.05	0.001144	3.10	0.0009677	3.15	0.0008164
3.20	0.0006872	3.25	0.0005771	3.30	0.0004835	3.35	0.0004041
3.40	0.0003370	3.45	0.0002803	3.50	0.0002327	3.55	0.0001927
3.60	0.0001591	3.65	0.0001312	3.70	0.0001078	3.75	0.00008844
3.80	0.00007237	3.85	0.00005908	3.90	0.00004812	3.95	0.00003909
4.00	**0.00003169**	4.05	0.00002562	4.10	0.00002067	4.15	0.00001663
4.20	0.00001335	4.25	0.00001070	4.30	0.00000855	4.35	0.00000681
4.40	0.00000542	4.45	0.00000430	4.50	0.00000340	4.55	0.00000268
4.60	0.00000211	4.65	0.00000166	4.70	0.00000130	4.75	0.00000102
4.80	0.00000079	4.85	0.00000062	4.90	0.00000048	4.95	0.00000037

FIGURE 7-7

Normal distribution, +1 sigma.
From Warren Brussee, *All About Six Sigma.*

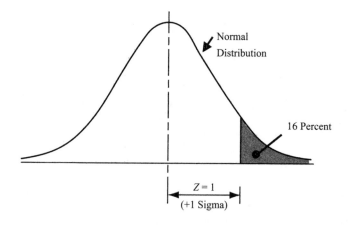

1.000 inch in diameter? (*Note:* The Z value is an indication of how many sigma, so in this case $Z = 2$.)

Looking at the standardized normal distribution table in Figure 7-6, $Z = 2$, $P = 0.02275$.

Answer: $P = 0.02275$, or 2.28 percent.

FIGURE 7-8

Normal distribution, ±1 sigma.
From Warren Brussee, *All About Six Sigma.*

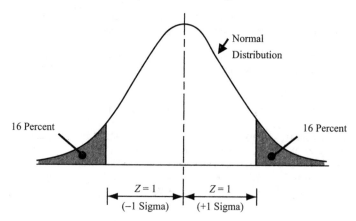

PROBLEM 9

What is the probability of finding a shaft not greater than 1.002 inch?

We first must realize that 1.002 inch is 2 sigma above nominal (since sigma = 0.001 inch), so $Z = 2$. Using the standardized normal distribution table in Figure 7-6 to get the probability, looking at $Z = 2$, we see that $P = 0.02275$.

Looking at the normal distribution curve at the top of the table (Figure 7-6), we can see that this P is the probability of being *greater than* 1.002 inches. Since we want *not greater than* 1.002 inches, we must subtract 0.02275 from 1.0000. Again, we know to do this because the total area under the curve, which represents all probabilities, equals 1. So $1 - 0.02275 = 0.97725$.

Answer: $P = 0.97725$, or 97.725 percent.

TIP
Assuming normal distribution

Use plotted data to check visually whether the data are normally distributed. When in doubt, plot more data. Unless the data are *dramatically* nonsymmetrical (data extremely off to one side) or *dramatically* bimodal (two lobes), assume a normal distribution. The data must *clearly* show a different distribution; if they do not, we assume the distribution is normal. Some computer programs use mathematical formulas to test whether data are normal, but optical inspection of the plotted data is generally sufficient. As you will see later, having a normal distribution allows you to directly use the absolute probability values in the standardized distribution table. However, if the distributions are *not* normal, the table values can still be used for comparison purposes.

As you will see in Chapter 8, most of the work we do in Six Sigma does not require a perfectly normal distribution because we are generally looking for relative change, not an absolute number based on the normal distribution table.

TIP
Normal distribution symmetry

Remembering that each half of the normal distribution curve is a mirror image of the other, we can use data given for the plus side to solve problems related to both sides.

PROBLEM 10

In the shaft process previously discussed, what is the probability of getting a shaft below 0.9978 inch in diameter?

This shaft diameter is 0.0022 inch below nominal (1 − 0.9978 inch). Since sigma = 0.0010 inch, this is 2.2 sigma below nominal, so $Z = 2.2$. Looking at the standardized normal distribution table (Figure 7-6), $Z = 2.2$, we see that $P = 0.0139$. Therefore, 1.39 percent of the data points would occur above a positive 2.2 sigma. Since the negative side of the probability table is a mirror image of the positive side, the probability also applies to a negative 2.2 sigma.

Answer: $P = .0139$, or 1.39 percent.

TIP

No values occur exactly at a Z point.

In using a standardized normal distribution curve, all values are assumed to be above or below a Z point. For example, if you wanted to know what percent of values are above $Z = 2$, it would be the same as the percent of values at or above $Z = 2$.

For simplicity, the previous shaft data had a sigma = 0.0010 inch. This was to make calculations and understanding easier. Usually the sigma doesn't correlate with the bin edges, nor is it such an even number. This in no way changes the logic or diminishes the value of the standardized normal distribution table (Figure 7-6), as shown in the following problems.

PROBLEM 11

Using the shaft example, let's assume that the customer has complained that the amount of variation in the shafts is causing process problems. The customer is especially critical of shafts less than 0.9980 inch and greater than 1.0020 inches (more than 0.0020 inch from nominal).

In response, the lathe is overhauled. On taking another 1,000 measurements after the overhaul, it is determined that the average has stayed at 1.0000 inch, but the sigma has been reduced from 0.0010 to 0.0007 inch.

The reduced sigma means that the variation between shafts is less than before the overhaul. We want to communicate to the customer what improvement he can expect in future shipments—specifically what reduction he will see in shafts more than 0.0020 inch above or below the nominal 1.0000-inch diameter.

Before the overhaul (Problem 8, sigma = 0.0010 inch), we found that the probability of finding a shaft at least 0.0020 inch above 1.0000 inch in diameter was 0.02275. Given that both sides of the curve are mirror images, we double that number to calculate the chances of being at least 0.0020 inch ± nominal:

$$P = 0.02275 \times 2 = 0.0455, \text{ or } 4.55 \text{ percent } (P \text{ before the overhaul}).$$

We must now calculate the P with the new reduced sigma (0.0007 inch). First, we see how many sigma "fit" between nominal and 0.0020 inch. We use the plus side first since that is the data given to us in the standardized normal distribution table (Figure 7-6).

We see that 0.0020 inch/0.0007 inch = 2.86 sigma fit. This gives us the Z to use in the standardized normal distribution table.

Using the standardized normal distribution table, looking at $Z = 2.85$ (the closest table data point), the P value we read from the table is 0.002186. So, 0.2186 percent of the shafts will be at least 0.0020 inch above nominal. We double this to include those at least 0.0020 inch below 1.0000-inch diameter:

$$2 \times 0.002186 = 0.004372$$

The total P is 0.004372, or 0.4372 percent (P after the overhaul).

Answer: Since the process had been making 4.55 percent at 0.0020 inch above or below 1.0000 inch and it is now making 0.4372 percent, the customer can expect to see 9.6 percent (0.437/4.55) of the former problem shafts.

PROBLEM 12

Let's change the above problem again to make it even more realistic. After the overhaul the lathe sigma is reduced to 0.0007 inch (same as above), but the average shaft diameter is now 1.0005 inches. The process plot is still normal. Will the customer be receiving less problem shafts than before the overhaul?

Since the process average is no longer centered at the 1.0000-inch nominal, the amount of product outside the 0.9980- to 1.0020-inch target is different for the large diameters than for the small diameters, so calculate each independently.

First, we will calculate the P for the too-large shafts. As before, we see how many sigma (0.0007 inch) fit between the new process average (1.0005 inch) and the +1.0020-inch upper limit:

(1.0020 inches − 1.0005 inches)/0.0007 inch = 2.143 sigma fit

Looking at the standardized normal distribution table (Figure 7-6), we see that the P at a Z of 2.15 (closest value to 2.143) is 0.01578. That means that 1.578 percent of the shafts will be 1.0020 inches in diameter or larger.

Looking at the too-small shafts, we do a similar calculation. First, find the value for the difference between the process average and the lower end of the target (the process average is 1.0005 inches and the lower target value is 0.9980 inch). The difference is 1.0005 inches − 0.9980 inch = 0.0025 inch.

We then see how many sigma (0.0007 inch) fit: 0.0025 inch/0.0007 inch = 3.57 sigma. Although we must use the data on the positive end of the curve, we know that the mirror image would be identical. Looking at the P value for a Z of 3.55, we get P = 0.0001927. So 0.019 percent of the shafts will be 0.9980 inch or smaller.

Answer: When we add the too-large and too-small diameter shafts, we get 1.578 percent + 0.019 percent = 1.60 percent of the shafts will be at least 0.0020 inch off the 1.0000-inch nominal. This 1.60 percent is less than the 4.45 percent the customer was receiving before the overhaul, so the customer will be receiving a better product. Note, however, that 1.60 percent is much higher than the 0.4372 percent (Problem 11) the customer would receive if the process were centered.

This change in both the average and the sigma is not unusual in a process change. However, it is usually not difficult to get the process mean back to the target center (in this case, 1.0000-inch diameter). If the process center is put back to nominal, we get the 10-fold improvement we saw in the earlier problem.

TIP

Adjusting the mean of a process versus reducing its sigma

Normally moving the mean of a process is easier than trying to reduce its sigma.

Changing a mean is often accomplished just by choosing the center around which the process will be run; it requires no major process change. A sigma reduction often requires a significant change in the process itself, like dramatically slowing the process or changing the equipment being used.

Note that in the above cases, the standardized normal distribution table (Figure 7-6) Z values that were used were those closest to the calculated values of Z. There was no attempt to extrapolate, or go to another table or computer program for greater accuracy. Either would have been possible, but if you look at the relative values obtained versus the changes being noted, the greater accuracy was not required. Often the calculation accuracy far exceeds the requirements of the output results.

TIP

Using Excel to get normal distribution values

Those wishing to use the computer to get the probability values for various values of Z can use Excel. After bringing up the Excel worksheet, click on *fx* Paste or Insert function in the toolbar. Under Category, click on Statistical. Then, under Function, click on NORMSDIST. When you enter a Z value, it gives you the probability values using the left end of the distribution as the reference zero, whereas the standardized normal distribution table (Figure 7-6) uses the right end of the distribution as zero. To convert either one to the other, simply subtract the value from 1.

For example, if you enter $Z = 2$ in the Excel NORMSDIST, you get a probability value of 0.97725. This is the probability of being less than the Z value. Thus, $1.00000 - 0.97725 = 0.02275$ is the probability of being greater than Z, which matches the probability given for $Z = 2$ on the standardized normal distribution table.

Just for information purposes, the Six Sigma process is sometimes referred to as "3 defects per million." If you look at the standardized normal distribution table (Figure 7-6), you will see that 3 defects per million is 4.5 sigma, not 6 sigma. The 6 sigma short-term target is tighter than the 4.5 sigma long-term goal because it assumes Motorola's 1.5 sigma process drift will take place over time, and allowance is made for this expected drift. The idea was that if you started with a process that was 6 sigma short term, you would have a 4.5 sigma process when the expected long-term drift was included, which would generate 3 defects per million products. This book does not recommend assuming the Motorola 1.5 sigma process drift because the actual long-term drift will vary substantially. This book recommends using short-term data for all calculations and therefore not having to allow for drift in your calculations. Techniques are offered in Chapter 9 on how long-term process drift can be monitored and minimized.

PLOTTING DATA

There are hundreds of computer programs available that will plot data and do some degree of statistical analysis. Some of these programs are quite good; many are somewhat confusing. This confusion problem stems from incomplete or confusing directions or help screens, the user's not taking the time to understand the details of the program, or even errors within the program.

Case Study: Blindly Using a Plotting Program

In a review of Six Sigma projects attended by green belts and black belts, the presenter was displaying what he described as "normal" data consisting of 100 individual data points, with the ±3 sigma lines as shown on the graph in Figure 7-9.

At the end of the presentation, one person asked how approximately 20 percent of the data points could be beyond the 3 sigma limits, since the limits were supposedly calculated from the data points displayed and 99.7 percent of the data points in a normal distribution are supposed to be within the ±3-sigma limits. This was an important question since the plotting program that was used for the graph was the designated statistical program for the whole corporation.

Only later did someone discover that within the program was a default that used the last 10 data points entered to calculate the 3 sigma limits.

This case study is problematic for several reasons. First, other than the questioner, no one else demonstrated a basic understanding of what the 3 sigma limits meant; no one else tested the graph for reasonableness. Second, it's troublesome that the default in the computer program would use only the last 10 points entered to calculate the 3 sigma limits (you will learn later that a *minimum* of 11 points is needed to get a decent estimate of sigma, with 30 points preferred). Third, almost no one using this program had bothered to understand how the program worked, or its defaults.

Many graphing programs are so forbidding that the user is just relieved to get an output. Many of these programs are powerful, but require care to use. Any user of statistical programs not completely familiar to them should do some manual work with the data before using the program. They should then input a very simplified set of data where they already know the outcome.

FIGURE 7-9

Plot of normal data consisting of 100 individual data points, based on 100 processed samples.
From Warren Brussee, *All About Six Sigma.*

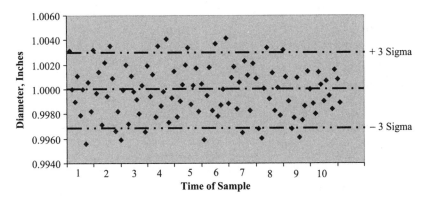

In this book we use Excel to generate our graphs. This is not because Excel is the best program for graphs, but because I'm assuming that most users of this text have Microsoft's Excel on their computers.

Using the Excel Graphing Program

I will go into more detail than you probably need in case you are not familiar with Excel. If you are completely familiar with graphing with Excel, you can quickly glance over this section.

First, make sure Excel's Data Analysis program is loaded into Tools on your computer. Bring up Microsoft Excel. On the header on the top of the screen, go to Tools. See if Data Analysis is one of the options available. If not, under Tools go to Add-ins. Check the boxes opposite Analysis ToolPak and Analysis ToolPak VBA, then OK. If either of these is not available, you will have to insert the Microsoft Office Professional disk and install them. You may have to completely close Excel then reopen it to see Data Analysis as one of the options. For now, go back out of Tools.

Copy the following 50 numbers into an Excel worksheet, column A.

1.0004	0.9996
0.9991	1.0008
1.0001	1.0005
0.9995	1
1.0012	0.9996
0.9998	0.9997
0.9986	0.9985
0.9999	0.9991
1.0000	1.0004
0.9996	0.9993
1.0002	1.0006
0.9988	0.9991
1.0009	1.0002

0.9994	1.0014
0.9978	1.0013
0.9982	0.9984
1.0015	0.9996
1.001	1.0009
1.0016	0.9998
0.999	0.9998
0.9989	0.9989
1.0001	0.9993
0.9972	1.0003
1.0009	1.0019
1.0024	0.9996

These numbers represent 50 shaft diameter readings we may expect from the previously discussed shaft process. After copying these numbers, highlight and then Order these numbers using the AZ down-arrow option in the second row header at the top of the screen. (If this option doesn't show, go into Data on the toolbar and you will see the AZ down arrow opposite Sort. Click on Ascending.) After ordering these, the top number will be 0.9972 and the bottom number will be 1.0024.

In column B, row 1, enter the formula = (bottom or maximum number) − (top or minimum number), which in this case will be = A50 − A1. This will give the difference between the largest and smallest shaft diameter, which will be 0.0052.

In that same column B, second row, insert the formula = 1.02 * B1/7. This gives us bin sizes for 7 bins. (See the following TIP for calculating the number of bins.) The 1.02 makes the total bin widths slightly wider than the data range. If we have more data, we can use more bins by changing the denominator from 7 to the higher bin quantity. With 7 bins, the bin width shown in B2 will be 0.0007577.

Now we have to show the specific bin edges. In C1, insert the formula = A1 − 0.01 * B1. In this example it will put a value of 0.99715 in C1. This gives the left bin edge, which is slightly less than the minimum data value. Then, in C2 insert the formula = C1 + B2. This determines that the next bin edge will be the number in C1 plus the bin width. C2 in this example will then be 0.99791. The $'s in this case "freeze" the bin width B2 for use in the next steps.

Under Edit, copy C2. Highlight C3 through C8 (you would highlight more if you had more bins). Then click Edit, Paste Special, and Formulas. This gives you the edge values for each of the remaining bins. In this example C8 should show bin value 1.00245, the right edge of the last bin. This value is slightly higher than the maximum data number.

Now, go to Tools in the top header, and click Data Analysis, and then Histogram. When this screen comes up, highlight column A (your data) and enter it as the Input Range. Then, click on the second box (Bin Range) and enter the highlighted bin ranges from column C. The options New Worksheet Ply and Chart Output should be chosen, then click OK. The histogram will come up. Drag down the right bottom corner to extend the vertical axis. The Histogram should look similar to the one in Figure 7-10.

FIGURE 7−10

Excel histogram.
From Warren Brussee, *All About Six Sigma.*

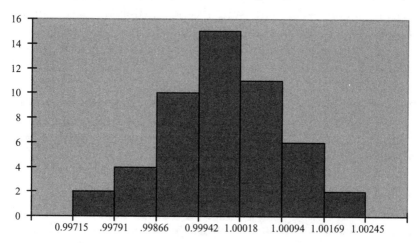

The bottom horizontal x axis, as labeled in Excel, makes it look like the bin values are in the middle of the bins rather than on the right edges. This was modified for the above illustration. Also, if you get more (or fewer) label digits than shown above, you can modify them to match the above (or whatever you desire) by formatting the bin-edge column in the Excel spreadsheet. You may want to add definition to the wording on the axis. However, in this book we are more interested in the histogram shape rather than in the labels.

TIP
Rule of thumb for the number of bins to use in a histogram

$$\text{\# of Bins} = \sqrt{\text{\# of Data Points}}$$

Note: This is only a general guideline. Feel free to experiment.

WHAT WE HAVE LEARNED IN CHAPTER 7

- Six Sigma work can't be done without some understanding of probability/statistics.
- Using basic probability techniques will help separate random results from assignable causes.
- Since the sum of the probabilities of all possible outcomes always equals 1, we can often use this knowledge to simplify a problem.
- Excel's BINOMDIST is sufficient for doing the probability calculations, using the cumulative function to save work in doing less-than or more-than calculations.
- Examine the data carefully to make sure they are truly independent.
- Because our confidence level is never 100 percent, any change must be verified with future tests or data. Past data can never completely validate a change.
- Plotting data is a step needed in implementing many of the Six Sigma tools.

- Using histograms to compare data helps spot unexpected differences and areas of opportunity. Using the standardized normal distribution table (Figure 7-6) to evaluate data on a normal distribution or to compare two processes with similarly shaped distributions can often help quantify a problem.
- Excel can be used to make histograms or get normal distribution values.

Testing for Statistically Significant Change

In Chapter 1, I suggested that healthcare costs could be reduced substantially with rigorous application of Six Sigma techniques. Patients and doctors should have valid comparative-effectiveness data to help them pick the best treatment option. The statistical techniques outlined in this chapter would be used for analyzing that comparative-effectiveness data.

TESTING FOR STATISTICALLY SIGNIFICANT CHANGE USING VARIABLES DATA

In this section you learn to use limited samples of variables data to make judgments on whether a population or process has changed. We will be comparing samples to the population and samples to each other.

The formulas in this section are used in the Define, Measure, Analysis, Improve, and Control steps in the DMAIC process. Here are some examples:

Manufacturing

Compare dimensional samples from two similar production lines, or compare shift samples on one line to look for significant differences.

Sales

Compare samples from different salespeople on sales dollars generated using samples from many random days.

Marketing

Compare samples of advertising dollars spent in a city over a period of time versus the sales generated in that city to see if advertising dollars make a significant difference in sales.

Accounting and Software Development

Sample error rates and look for differences among people doing similar work, using samples from many individual days.

Receivables

Check for correlations between sample delinquent receivables and the Dun & Bradstreet (D&B) rating. Use data from many individual days.

Insurance

Sample costs among different treatment centers on similar procedures, using data from many individual days. Compare costs/effectiveness of different treatments in the same facility.

In the discussion in Chapter 7 on probability, we learned to judge whether an event was due to random or assignable cause. In all cases we knew the odds of the random event, like 0.5 on a coin flip or 1/6 on rolling a die. An event that was nonrandom hinted at a problem or an opportunity.

In the section on data plots and distributions in Chapter 7, we plotted a large quantity of data from a sample or population to see trends or changes. We would use the plot to see the data distribution. We used a standardized normal distribution chart to perform further analysis. Once we had an identified distribution, we used this knowledge to judge whether an event was due to random or assignable cause.

Similarly, in this chapter we do statistical tests on variables data to determine if a change is large enough to be significant at a 95 percent confidence level.

DEFINITION

Variables data   Variables data are measurable and generally in decimal form. Theoretically you could look at enough decimal places to find that no two values are exactly the same. *Continuous data* is another term used for this type of data. The resolution of variables data measurements should be such that at least 10 possible data "steps" are within the tolerance or area of interest.

TIP

Sample size rule of thumb on variables data

To calculate sigma on variables data, a rule-of-thumb minimum sample size n of 11 is needed, with a preferable sample size n of 30 or more.

To calculate an average, the sample size n can be as low as 5. But, since we normally must calculate sigma at the same time, a minimum n of 11 and preferable n of 30 is the standard.

This rule of thumb should only be used when it is not possible to calculate a specific minimum sample size. This situation would exist where we did not know the population sigma or were not sure of the accuracy we needed.

Almost any formal or informal quality system has a sample size that is used to make decisions. Even where there are no formal rules, someone makes a judgment on how many items should be reviewed before making a determination. This is true in reviewing office staff output, incoming product, medical errors, accounting errors, programming mistakes, and so on. If too many examples are required, costs are increased, a decision is delayed, and any action on poor performance is also delayed. If a judgment is made on too small of a sample, then erroneous calls are often made.

DEFINITION

Labeling averages and standard deviations   To label the average of a population, we use $\bar{X}$; to label the sample averages, we use $\bar{x}$.

Similarly, the standard deviation (sigma) of the population is labeled S and the sample standard deviations s.

We will use $\bar{X}$, S, $\bar{x}$, and s in this book rather than the Greek letters used in some texts. Both forms are in use and acceptable.

DEFINITION

Population versus sample   We seldom have *all* the data on a population, so we make an estimate about the population based on large or multiple samples.

TIP

Two methods of estimating $\bar{x}$ and S

1. **Estimating the population $\bar{X}$ and S from a large sample.** You can estimate a population average $\bar{X}$ and sigma S from the $\bar{x}$ and s of a large sample that has a minimum sample size of $n = 30$. Assume that the population average and sigma are the same as that of the large sample.

2. **Estimating the population $\bar{X}$ and S from multiple samples of similar size n.** Use the following formula:

$$\bar{X} = \frac{x_1 + x_2}{2}$$

$\bar{X}$ = population average
$\bar{x}_1$ = average from sample 1
$\bar{x}_2$ = average from sample 2

$$S = \sqrt{\frac{s_1^2 + s_2^2}{2}}$$

S = population sigma
s_1 = sigma of sample 1
s_2 = sigma of sample 2

If you have three or more samples, modify the formulas accordingly, with more sample sigmas or averages in the numerator and dividing by the total number of samples.

Example: If you have $s_1 = 16$ and $s_2 = 12$, then:

$$S = \sqrt{\frac{s_1^2 + s_2^2}{2}} = \sqrt{\frac{16^2 + 12^2}{2}} = 14.14$$

If the sample sizes are substantially different, use the s from the largest sample for the estimate of S, since the confidence related to a small sample is suspect. You can also use a computer program that will compensate for different sample sizes, but this is not normally necessary.

PROBLEM 1

You have data from two samples taken from a stable process, with no other knowledge of the process population:

Sample #1	Sample #2
$n = 15$	$n = 42$
$\bar{x} = 15.05$	$\bar{x} = 15.38$
$s = 1.58$	$s = 1.46$

What is the estimate for the population average $\bar{X}$ and sigma S?

Since the sample sizes n are quite different from each other, use the larger sample. Also, since the sample size of #2 is over 30, we feel comfortable that it is a reasonable estimate. So the estimate for the population is:

$$\bar{X} = 15.38$$
$$S = 1.46$$

PROBLEM 2

You have data from three samples taken from a stable process, with no other knowledge of the process population.

Sample #1	Sample #2	Sample #3
$n = 16$	$n = 18$	$n = 15$
$\bar{x_1} = 14.96$	$\bar{x_2} = 15.05$	$\bar{x_3} = 15.04$
$s_1 = 1.52$	$s_2 = 1.49$	$s_3 = 1.53$

What is the estimate for the population average $\bar{X}$ and sigma S?

Since all three samples have a similar sample size n, we will use the above formulas to calculate our estimate for the population.

$$\bar{X} = \frac{\overline{x_1} + \overline{x_2} + \overline{x_3}}{3}$$

$$\bar{X} = \frac{14.96 + 15.05 + 15.04}{3} = 15.017$$

$$S = \sqrt{\frac{s_1^2 + s_2^2 + s_3^2}{3}}$$

$$S = \sqrt{\frac{1.52^2 + 1.49^2 + 1.53^2}{3}}$$

$$S = \sqrt{\frac{6.8714}{3}} = 1.513$$

TIP

Maximize the sample size to estimate the population average and sigma.

The greater the sample size n ("n is your friend"), the better your estimate of the population average and standard deviation.

FORMULA: Calculating minimum sample size and sensitivity on variables data

Use the following formula to calculate minimum sample size on variables data.

$$n = \left(\frac{Z * S}{h} \right)^2$$

n = minimum sample size on variables data (Always round up.)
Z = confidence level (When in doubt use $Z = 1.96$, as in the following tip.)

> S = population standard deviation
>
> h = smallest change we want to be able to sense
>
> (When in doubt, use h = total tolerance/10, or h = 0.6S.)
>
> Note that the formula shown above can be rewritten as:
>
> $$h = \sqrt{\frac{Z^2 * S^2}{n}}$$
>
> This allows us to calculate what sensitivity h (change) we can sense with a given sample size and confidence level.

A lot of judgment goes into calculating sample size. Often the final sample size will be a compromise between cost (both product and inspection) and customer need. The formulas allow you to make sample size a knowledge-based decision rather than just a guess.

Looking at the components of the sample size formula, we see that the sample size n is not only influenced by the sensitivity (h) required but also by the process sigma. Sometimes this formula will point out that the sample size requirement is so excessive that only a process improvement (reduced sigma) or a loosening of the customer's requirements (increased h) will make sampling viable. The alternatives to sampling include automatic inspection or 100 percent process sorting. This use of the sample size formulas to understand these options is a very productive use of the Six Sigma process.

TIP

Z, confidence of results

Z relates to the probability, or confidence, we are looking for. For one-tailed questions (like greater-than), use Z = 1.64 for 95 percent confidence. On two-tailed problems (like greater than *or* less than), use Z = 1.96 for 95 percent confidence.

We normally test to a 95 percent confidence.

Assume a problem is two-tailed unless it has been described specifically as one-tailed. *So the Z will normally be 1.96.*

You can find countless tables and computer programs that will test significance at many different confidence levels.

If you recall from Chapter 7, running two tests at a 0.95 probability minimizes "chance" to $p = 0.05 \times 0.05 = 0.0025$. There is normally no reason to test to a higher confidence than 95 percent since you usually have to rerun any test to see if the results replicate.

PROBLEM 3

Administrators at a high school had just gotten the results from a national achievement test, and they wanted to know how many random results they would have to review before deciding, with 95 percent confidence, whether the performance of the students had changed. The historical sigma on this test was 1.24. They wanted to be able to sense a change of $0.6S$, which is 0.744.

$$n = \left(\frac{Z * S}{h} \right)^2$$

$$n = \left(\frac{1.96 * 1.24}{0.744} \right)^2$$

$$n = 10.67$$

So they would have to look at the results from at least 11 tests to see if the performance had changed 0.744, with a 95 percent confidence.

PROBLEM 4

Administrators at a high school had just gotten the results from a national achievement test, and they wanted to know how many random results they would have to review before deciding, with a 95 percent confidence, whether the performance of the students had improved. The historical sigma on this test was 1.24. They wanted to be able to sense an improvement of $0.6S$, which is 0.744.

Note that this problem is now one-tailed because they only want to see if the students improved. This changes the value of Z to 1.64.

$$n = \left(\frac{Z * S}{h}\right)^2$$

$$n = \left(\frac{1.64 * 1.24}{0.744}\right)^2$$

$$n = 7.47$$

So they would have to look at the results from at least 8 tests to see if the performance had improved 0.744, with a 95 percent confidence.

Note that by only looking for improved scores, the minimum sample size is reduced from 11 to 8. However, knowing if change occurred only on the up side is usually not sufficient because the school would at some point be concerned about change on both the up and down sides. Because of this, the sample size is usually determined by a two-tailed $Z = 1.96$, as in Problem 3, giving a minimum sample size of 11.

PROBLEM 5

Before doing the calculations in Problems 3 and 4, someone had already tabulated the results from 20 tests. At 95 percent confidence, what change in results h could be sensed from reviewing this many results versus the minimum 0.744 change target? The historical sigma on this test was 1.24.

$$h = \sqrt{\frac{Z^2 * S^2}{n}}$$

$$h = \sqrt{\frac{1.96^2 * 1.24^2}{20}}$$

$$h = 0.543$$

So the sensitivity on 20 results is 0.543 versus the 0.744 target. The school would be able to sense a smaller change.

This shows the benefit of a larger sample size $n = 20$ versus $n = 11$.

USING A SAMPLE TO CHECK FOR A CHANGE VERSUS A POPULATION

We will use a three-step process:

1. First check the distributions to see if the data histogram shapes (population versus sample) are substantially different.
2. If the distribution shapes are not substantially different, then see if the sigmas are significantly different.
3. If neither of the above tests shows a difference, we then check if the averages are significantly different.

If we sense a significant difference at any point in the above steps, we stop and try to find the cause. Any significant difference is potentially important since it can affect costs, quality, and so on.

TIP
Don't use data analysis alone to drive decisions.

The following formulas will give you the ability to detect change. The reaction to any analytical finding should be tempered by common sense and expert knowledge. This should not stop you from pursuing a finding that violates common sense or expert knowledge because it is not uncommon to discover that some preconceived notions are invalid. However, tread softly because the analysis could also be wrong.

Remember, we are testing to a 95 percent confidence level, which means that 5 percent of the time you could be wrong. And, the 5 percent is optimistic. That is the mathematical error. You have gauge error, sampling error, and other types of error that are in addition to the 5 percent error. Probably 10 percent is a more realistic estimate of actual possible error.

That is why an additional test under controlled conditions is always needed to validate a finding.

Step 1. Checking the Distributions

First, it may be necessary to plot a large number of individual measurements to verify that the sample distribution shape is similar to that of the earlier population. Although a process distribution will normally be similar over time, it is important to verify this, especially when running a test or after a policy change, machine wreck, personnel change, and so on. We are only concerned about gross differences, like one plot being very strongly skewed or bimodal versus the other. If plotting is required, you will need a sample size of at least 36. If there is a substantial change in the distribution shape, there is no reason to do further tests because we know the process has changed and we should be trying to understand the change cause and ramifications.

If there are outliers (data values clearly separate from the general distribution), you must determine the causes of those data points before doing any quantitative statistical analysis on the data. If you can confidently determine that the questionable data points are due to an error in collecting or entering data and they don't reflect the process, then you can remove the data points. If the wild data points are *not* an input error, then you have found a potential problem that must be resolved.

TIP
Examining plotted data

Visually examining plotted data will often give insights that can't be seen with any quantitative method.

Here is an example showing why you can't just look at the numerical statistics, and why you first have to examine the plotted data. Below are two sets of 50 pieces of data, with the averages and standard deviations shown below each set of data. Notice that the averages and standard deviations of both groups of data are basically the same.

Data Set 1

0.9991	0.9991	0.9998	1.0009
0.9978	0.9993	1.0002	1.0009
0.9982	0.9993	1.0002	1.001
0.9984	0.9994	1.0003	1.001
0.9985	0.9995	1.0003	1.0012
0.9986	0.9996	1.0003	1.0013
0.9988	0.9996	1.0004	1.0014
0.9989	0.9996	1.0004	1.0015
0.9989	0.9996	1.0005	1.0015
0.999	0.9996	1.0006	1.0015
0.999	0.9998	1.0006	1.0016
0.9991	0.9998	1.0008	
0.9972	0.9998	1.0009	

Average = 0.999892

Standard deviation = 0.00105

Data Set 2

0.9992	0.9993	1.0000	0.9995
0.9992	0.9993	0.9995	1.0000
0.9992	0.9993	0.9995	1.0000
0.9992	0.9993	0.9996	1.0000
0.9993	0.9993	1.0000	1.0000
0.9993	0.9994	1.0000	1.0002
1.0000	0.9994	0.9993	1.0034
0.9993	0.9994	1.0000	1.0025
0.9993	0.9994	1.0000	1.003
0.9993	1.0000	0.9994	1.0032
0.9993	0.9994	1.0000	1.0021
0.9993	0.9994	1.0000	
0.9993	0.9995	1.0000	

Average = 0.999896

Standard deviation = 0.00105

Now we want to look at the data plots, shown in Figures 8-1 and 8-2, for both sets of data.

Note that the data distributions have completely different shapes. The distributions don't just have a wider spread; nor do their centers just change. They have a totally different shape.

These processes cannot be compared using standard numerical tests because they are two completely different processes. They might have been the same processes at some time in the past—at least you thought they were, otherwise you probably wouldn't be comparing them now. However, due to a machine wreck or an unknown process change, they are no longer similar. Trying to compare them now is like comparing apples to oranges. This difference cannot be seen

FIGURE 8−1

Data plots for data set 1.
From Warren Brussee, *All About Six Sigma*.

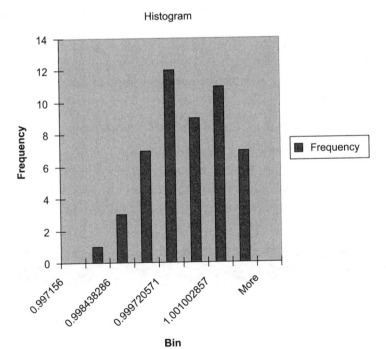

FIGURE 8-2

Data plots for data set 2.
From Warren Brussee, *All About Six Sigma.*

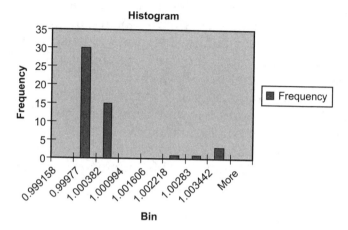

by just looking at the data averages and standard deviations; plotting is required.

Note that discovering this difference is usually a good thing, because it often gives insight to some process deviation or change that was unknown and should be addressed.

Step 2. Checking the Sigmas

If the process distribution has not changed qualitatively (looking at the data plots), then you can do some quantitative tests. The first thing to check is if the sigma has changed significantly. The sigma on a process does not normally change unless a basic

FORMULA: Chi-square test of a sample sigma *s* versus a population sigma *S*

$$\mathrm{Chi}_t^2 = \frac{(n-1)s^2}{S^2}$$

n = sample size

s = sample sigma

S = population sigma

We compare the calculated Chi_t^2 results to the values in the simplified chi-square distribution table provided in Figure 8-3. If the Chi_t^2 test value we calculated is less than the table low value or greater than the table high value, we are 95 percent confident that the sample sigma s is different from the sigma S of the population.

change in the process has occurred. To see if the sigma has changed, we calculate a chi-square test value, Chi_t^2.

If there has been a significant change in the sigma, there would be no reason to do further tests, and we should be trying to understand the change cause and ramifications.

Step 3. Checking the Averages

If in steps 1 and 2 we have not found that either the distribution or sigma has changed significantly, we are then free to test whether the sample average is significantly different from the population average. We will have to calculate a t-test value, t_t, to compare to a value in the simplified t distribution table in Figure 8-4.

FORMULA: t test of a population average $\overline{X}$ versus a sample average $\overline{x}$

$$t_t = \frac{|\overline{x} - \overline{X}|}{\dfrac{s}{\sqrt{n}}}$$

$\overline{X}$ = population average

$\overline{x}$ = sample average

s = sample sigma

n = sample size

$|\overline{x} - \overline{X}|$ is the absolute value of the difference of the averages, so ignore a minus sign in the difference.

We compare this calculated t-test (t_t) value against the value in the simplified t distribution table in Figure 8-4. If our calculated t-test (t_1) value value is greater than the value in the table, then we are 95 percent confident that the sample average is significantly different than the population average.

FIGURE 8-3

Simplified chi-square distribution table to test a sample sigma *s* (with sample size *n*) versus a population sigma *S*. From Warren Brussee, *All About Six Sigma*.

	95% Confident They Are Different If Chi_t^2 Is			95% Confident They Are Different If Chi_t^2 Is	
	< Low	Or > High		< Low	Or > High
n	Low Test	High Test	*n*	Low Test	High Test
6	0.831209	12.83249	36	20.56938	53.20331
7	1.237342	14.44935	37	21.33587	54.43726
8	1.689864	16.01277	38	22.10562	55.66798
9	2.179725	17.53454	39	22.87849	56.89549
10	2.700389	19.02278	40	23.6543	58.12005
11	3.246963	20.4832	41	24.43306	59.34168
12	3.815742	21.92002	42	25.21452	60.56055
13	4.403778	23.33666	43	25.99866	61.77672
14	5.008738	24.73558	44	26.78537	62.99031
15	5.628724	26.11893	45	27.57454	64.20141
16	6.262123	27.48836	46	28.36618	65.41013
17	6.907664	28.84532	47	29.16002	66.61647
18	7.564179	30.19098	48	29.95616	67.82064
19	8.230737	31.52641	49	30.7545	69.02257
20	8.906514	32.85234	50	31.55493	70.22236
21	9.590772	34.16958	55	35.58633	76.19206
22	10.28291	35.47886			
23	10.98233	36.78068	60	39.66185	82.11737
24	11.68853	38.07561			
25	12.40115	39.36406	65	43.77594	88.00398
26	13.11971	40.6465	70	47.92412	93.85648
27	13.84388	41.92314			
28	14.57337	43.19452	80	56.30887	105.4727
29	15.30785	44.46079			
30	16.04705	45.72228	90	64.79339	116.989
31	16.79076	46.97922	100	73.3611	128.4219
32	17.53872	48.23192			
33	18.29079	49.48044			
34	19.04666	50.7251			
35	19.80624	51.96602			

FIGURE 8 − 4

Simplified t distribution table to compare a sample average (size = n) with a population average or to compare two samples of size n_1 and n_2, using $n = (n_1 + n_2 - 1)$. From Warren Brussee, *All About Six Sigma*.

95% Confidence (Assumes Two-Tailed)			
If the calculated t_t-test value exceeds the table t value, then the two averages being compared are significantly different.			
n	**t value**	**n**	**t value**
6	2.571	31	2.042
7	2.447	32	2.04
8	2.365	33	2.037
9	2.306	34	2.035
10	2.262	35	2.032
11	2.228	36	2.03
12	2.201	37	2.028
13	2.179	38	2.026
14	2.16	39	2.024
15	2.145	40	2.023
16	2.131	45	2.015
17	2.12		
18	2.11	50	2.01
19	2.101		
20	2.093	60	2.001
21	2.086	70	1.995
22	2.08		
23	2.074	80	1.99
24	2.069		
25	2.064	90	1.987
26	2.06	100+	1.984
27	2.056		
28	2.052		
29	2.048		
30	2.045		

PROBLEM 6

We have made a process change on our infamous lathe that is machining shafts. We want to know, with 95 percent confidence, if the "before" process, with an average $\bar{X}$ of 1.0003 inches and a sigma S of 0.00170 inch, has changed.

We use our three-step process to look for change. Assume that we first plotted some data from after the change and compared it with a plot of data before the change and saw no large differences in the shape of the two distributions. We must now compare the sigma before and after the change.

What is the minimum sample size we need, assuming we want to be able to see a change h of $0.6S$?

$h = 0.6S = 0.6 \times 0.00170$ inch $= 0.00102$ inch

$Z = 1.96$

$S = 0.00170$ inch

$$n = \left(\frac{Z*S}{h} \right)^2$$

$$n = \left(\frac{1.96*0.00170''}{0.00102''} \right)^2$$

$n = 11$ (rounding up)

Now that we know the minimum sample size, we can take the sample.

We want to know if the sample sigma is significantly different from the "before" population sigma. Assume that, from the sample, we calculate $s = 0.00173$ inch.

$n = 11$

$s = 0.00173$ inch

$S = 0.00170$ inch

$$\text{Chi}_t^2 = \frac{(n-1)s^2}{S^2} = \frac{(11-1)0.00173''^2}{0.00170''^2} = 10.356$$

Looking at the simplified chi-square distribution table in Figure 8-3, with $n = 11$, the low value is 3.24696 and the high value is 20.4832. Since our test value 10.356 is not outside that range, we can't say that the sigma of the sample is different (at 95 percent confidence) from the population sigma.

Since we were not able to see a difference in the distribution or the sigma, we will now see if the averages are significantly different. Assume that the after-change sample ($n = 11$) had an average $\bar{x}$ of 0.9991 inch.

$$\bar{x} = 0.9991 \text{ inch}$$

$$\bar{X} = 1.0003 \text{ inch}$$

$$s = 0.00173 \text{ inch}$$

$$n = 11$$

$$t_t = \frac{\left|\bar{x} - \bar{X}\right|}{\dfrac{s}{\sqrt{n}}}$$

$$t_t = \frac{\left|0.9991'' - 1.0003''\right|}{\dfrac{0.00173''}{\sqrt{11}}} = 2.3005$$

Looking at the simplified t distribution table in Figure 8-4, with $n = 11$, our calculated t-test value 2.3005 is greater than the table value (opposite $n = 11$: 2.228). We therefore assume that, with 95 percent confidence, the sample average *is* significantly different from the population.

The average has changed significantly from what it was before. We should therefore decide whether the process change was detrimental and should be reversed. Here is where judgment must be used, but you have data to help.

CHECKING FOR A STATISTICALLY SIGNIFICANT CHANGE BETWEEN TWO SAMPLES

We sometimes want to compare samples from two similar processes or from one process at different times. As we did when comparing a sample to a population, we do three steps in checking for a change between two samples.

1. Check the distributions to see if they are substantially different.
2. If the distribution shapes are not substantially different, then see if the sigmas are significantly different.
3. If neither of the above tests shows a difference, then check if the averages are significantly different.

Knowing whether there is a difference at any of the above steps is important since it may affect costs, quality, and so on.

Step 1. Checking the Distributions

First, it may be necessary to plot a large number of individual measurements to verify that the sample distribution shapes are similar. Although a process distribution will normally be similar over time, it is important to verify this, especially when running a test, after a policy change, machine wreck, personnel change, and so on. We are only concerned about gross differences, like one plot being very strongly skewed or bimodal versus the other. If plotting is required, a sample size of at least 36 will be needed. If there is a substantial change in the distribution, we know the process has changed and we should be trying to understand the change cause and ramifications.

Step 2. Checking the Sigmas

If the sample distributions have not changed qualitatively (looking at the data plots), then you can do some quantitative tests. The first thing to check is whether the sigma has changed significantly. The sigma on a process does not normally change unless a substantial basic change in the process has occurred. To see if the sigma has changed we do an F test, F_t.

FORMULA: F test comparing the sigmas s of two samples

$$F_t = \frac{s_1^2}{s_2^2} \text{ (Put the larger } s \text{ quantity on top, as the numerator.)}$$

---

s_1 = sample with the larger sigma

s_2 = sample with the smaller sigma

The sample sizes n should be within 20 percent of each other. There are tables and programs that allow for greater differences, but since you control sample sizes and get more reliable results with similar sample sizes, these other tables and programs are generally not needed.

Compare this F_t to the value in the simplified F table in Figure 8-5. If the F_t value exceeds the table F value, then the sigmas are significantly different.

PROBLEM 7

Suppose that in our now-familiar shaft example we take two samples. They could be from one lathe or two different lathes doing the same job. We have already plotted the samples and found that the shapes of the distributions were not substantially different. We now want to know if the sample sigmas are significantly different with 95 percent confidence.

Sample 1	Sample 2
$\overline{x_1}$ = 0.9982 inch	$\overline{x_2}$ = 1.0006 inch
s_1 = 0.00273 inch	s_2 = 0.00162 inch
n_1 = 21	n_2 = 19

To check the sigmas to see if the two processes are significantly different, we calculate the F-test value and compare this to the value in the simplified F table (Figure 8-5).

Since our sample sizes are within 20 percent of each other, we can use the previous formula.

$$F_t = \frac{s_1^2}{s_2^2} = \frac{0.00273''^2}{0.00162''^2} = 2.840$$

We now compare 2.840 to the value in the simplified F table (Figure 8-5). Use the average $n = 20$ to find the table value, which is 2.17. Since our calculated value is greater

FIGURE 8-5

Simplified F table (95% confidence) to compare sigmas from two samples (sizes n_1 and n_2, sample sizes equal within 20%) $n = \dfrac{n_1 + n_2}{2}$.

From Warren Brussee, *All About Six Sigma*.

If the calculated F_t value exceeds the table value, assume a significant difference.				
n	*F*		*n*	*F*
6	5.05		31	1.84
7	4.28		32	1.82
8	3.79		33	1.8
9	3.44		34	1.79
10	3.18		35	1.77
11	2.98		36	1.76
12	2.82		37	1.74
13	2.69		38	1.73
14	2.58		39	1.72
15	2.48		40	1.7
16	2.4		42	1.68
17	2.33		44	1.66
18	2.27		46	1.64
19	2.22		48	1.62
20	2.17		50	1.61
21	2.12		60	1.54
22	2.08		70	1.49
23	2.05		80	1.45
24	2.01		100	1.39
25	1.98		120	1.35
26	1.96		150	1.31
27	1.93		200	1.26
28	1.9		300	1.21
29	1.88		400	1.18
30	1.86		500	1.16
			750	1.13
			1000	1.11
			2000	1.08

than the table value, we can say with 95 percent confidence that the two processes' sigmas are different. We must now decide what the cause and ramifications are of this change in the sigma.

PROBLEM 8

Suppose that in our shaft example we take two different samples. The samples could be from one lathe or two different lathes doing the same job.

We have already plotted the samples and found that the distributions are not substantially different. We now want to know if the sample sigmas are significantly different with 95 percent confidence.

Sample 1	Sample 2
$\overline{x_1} = 0.9982$ inch	$\overline{x_2} = 1.0006$ inches
$s_1 = 0.00193$ inch	$s_2 = 0.00162$ inch
$n_1 = 21$	$n_2 = 19$

Calculating an F_t:

$$F_t = \frac{s_1^2}{s_2^2} = \frac{0.00193^2}{0.00162^2} = 1.42$$

We now compare 1.42 to the value in the simplified F table (Figure 8-5). Use the average $n = 20$ to find the table value, which is 2.17. Since 1.42 is less than the table value of 2.17, we can't say with 95 percent confidence that the processes are different (with regard to their sigmas).

We now test to see if the two sample averages are significantly different.

Step 3. Checking the Averages

Since we did *not* find that either the distribution shape or sigma had changed, we now test whether the two sample averages are significantly different. We calculate a t-test value (t_t) to compare to a value in the simplified t distribution table (Figure 8-4).

FORMULA: t test of two sample averages $\overline{x_1}$ and x_2

$$t_t = \frac{\left|\overline{X_1} - \overline{X_2}\right|}{\sqrt{\left(\dfrac{n_1 s_1^2 + n_2 s_2^2}{n_1 + n_2}\right)\left(\dfrac{1}{n_1} + \dfrac{1}{n_2}\right)}}$$

$\overline{X_1}$ and $\overline{X_2}$ are two sample averages

s_1 and s_2 are the sigmas on the two samples

n_1 and n_2 are the two sample sizes

$\left|\overline{X_1} - \overline{X_2}\right|$ is the absolute difference between the averages, ignoring a minus sign in the difference.

We then compare this calculated t-test value against the value in the simplified t table (Figure 8-4). If our calculated t-test number is greater than the value in the table, then we are 95 percent confident that the sample averages are significantly different.

Returning to the samples in Problem 8, we must calculate our t test (t_t):

Sample 1

$\overline{X_1}$ = 0.9982 inch

s_1 = 0.00193 inch

n_1 = 21

Sample 2

$\overline{X_2}$ = 1.0006 inches

s_2 = 0.00162 inch

n_2 = 19

$$t_t = \frac{\left|\overline{X_1} - \overline{X_2}\right|}{\sqrt{\left(\dfrac{n_1 s_1^2 + n_2 s_2^2}{n_1 + n_2}\right)\left(\dfrac{1}{n_1} + \dfrac{1}{n_2}\right)}}$$

$$t_t = \frac{\left|0.9982'' - 1.0006''\right|}{\sqrt{\left(\dfrac{21(0.00193'')^2 + 19(0.00162'')^2}{21 + 19}\right)\left(\dfrac{1}{21} + \dfrac{1}{19}\right)}} = 4.24$$

We now compare this 4.24 with the value from the simplified t distribution table (Figure 8-4). (Use $n = n_1 + n_2 - 1 = 39$.) Since the calculated 4.24 is greater than the table value of 2.024, we can conclude with 95 percent confidence that the two process means are significantly different.

We would normally want to find out why and decide what we are going to do with this knowledge.

> **TIP**
> Tests on averages and sigmas never prove "sameness."
>
> The chi-square, F, and t tests test only for significant difference. If these tests do not show a significant difference, it does not prove that the two samples or the sample and population are identical. It just means that with the amount of data we have, we can't conclude with 95 percent confidence that they are different. *Confidence tests never prove that two things are the same.*

INCIDENTAL STATISTICS TERMINOLOGY NOT USED IN PRECEDING TESTS

You will not find the term *null hypothesis* used in the above confidence tests, but it is inferred by the way the tests are done. Null hypothesis is a term that is often used in statistics books to mean that your base assumption is that nothing (null) changed. (An analogy is someone being assumed innocent until proven guilty.) This assumption is included in the above tests.

Several of the tables used in this book are titled as "simplified." This includes the chi square, F, and t tables. The main simplification relates to the column showing sample size *n*. In most other statistics books, the equivalent chi-square, F, and t tables label this column as *degrees of freedom*. One statistics book states that *degrees of freedom* is one of the most difficult terms in statistics to describe. The statistics book then goes on to show that, in almost all cases, degrees of freedom is equivalent to $n - 1$. This therefore becomes the knee-jerk translation ($n - 1$ = degrees of freedom) of almost everyone using tables with degrees of freedom.

The chi-square, F, and t tables in this book are shown with the $n-1$ equivalency built in. This was done to make life easier. In the extremely rare cases where degrees of freedom are not equivalent to $n-1$, the resultant error will be trivial versus the accuracy requirements of the results. The validity of your Six Sigma test results will not be compromised.

You may need this ($n-1$ = degrees of freedom) equivalency if you refer to other tables or use software with degrees of freedom requested.

TESTING FOR STATISTICALLY SIGNIFICANT CHANGE USING PROPORTIONAL DATA

In this section we will learn to use limited samples on proportional data. The discussion will parallel the previous section, in which we learned to use limited samples on variables data. Valid sampling and analysis of proportional data may be needed in all steps in the DMAIC process.

When a news report discusses the latest poll taken on 1,000 people related to two presidential hopefuls, and one candidate gets 51 percent and the other 49 percent of the polled preferences, a knowledgeable news reporter will not say that that one candidate is slightly ahead. This is because the poll results are merely an *estimate* on the overall population's choice for president and the sample poll results have to be significantly different before any conclusion can be made as to what the total population is expected to vote. In this section you will learn how large of a sample is required and what difference in sample results is needed before we can predict, with 95 percent confidence, that there are true differences in a population. Here are some examples of how this information is used:

Manufacturing

Use samples of scrap parts to calculate proportions on shifts or similar production lines. Look for statistically significant differences in scrap rate.

Sales

Sample and compare proportions of successful sales by different salespeople.

Marketing

Use polls to prioritize where advertising dollars should be spent.

Accounting and Software Development

Use samples to compare error rates of groups or individuals.

Receivables

Sample overdue receivables, then compare proportions versus due dates on different product lines. Adjust prices on products with statistically different overdue receivables.

Insurance

Sample challenged claims versus total claims in different groups, then compare proportions. Adjust group prices accordingly.

DEFINITION

Proportional data   Proportional data are based on attribute inputs such as good or bad or yes or no. Examples are the proportion of defects in a process, proportion of yes votes for a candidate, and the proportion of students failing a test.

   Proportional data can also be based on "stepped" numerical data, where the measurements steps are too wide to use as attribute data.

TIP

Because of the large sample sizes required when using proportional data, if possible, use variables data instead.

When people are interviewed regarding their preference in an upcoming election, the outcome of the sampling is proportional data. The interviewer asks whether a person is intending to vote for a candidate, yes or no. After polling many people, the pollsters tabulate the proportion of yes (or no) results versus the total of people surveyed. This kind of data requires very large sample sizes. That is why pollsters state that, based on polling over 1,000 people; the predictions are accurate within 3 percent, or ±3 percent (with 95 percent confidence). We will be able to validate this with the following sample-size formula.

FORMULA: Calculating minimum sample size and sensitivity on proportional data

$$n = \left(\frac{1.96\sqrt{(p)(1-p)}}{h} \right)^2$$

n = sample size of attribute data, like good and bad (95 percent confidence)

p = probability of an event (the proportion of bad in a sample, chance of getting elected, and so on). (When in doubt, use $p = 0.5$, the most conservative.)

h = sensitivity, or accuracy required. (For example, for predicting elections it may be ±3 percent or $h = 0.03$. Another guideline is to be able to sense 10 percent of the tolerance or difference between the proportions.)

Note that the formula shown above can be rewritten:

$$h = 1.96\sqrt{\frac{(p)(1-p)}{n}}$$

This allows us to see what sensitivity h we will be able to sense at a given sample size and probability.

Let's do an election example. If the most recent polls show that a candidate has a 20 percent chance of getting elected, we may use $p = 0.2$. We will want an accuracy of ± 3 percent of the total vote, so $h = 0.03$.

$p = 0.2$

$h = 0.03$

$$n = \left(\frac{1.96\sqrt{(p)(1-p)}}{h} \right)^2$$

$$n = \left(\frac{1.96\sqrt{(0.2)(1-0.2)}}{.03} \right)^2$$

$n = 682.95$

So we would have to poll 683 (rounding up) people to get an updated probability on someone whose estimated chance of being elected was 20 percent in earlier polls. However, if we had no polls to estimate a candidate's chances or we wanted to be the most conservative, we would use $p = 0.5$.

$p = 0.5$

$h = 0.03$

$$n = \left(\frac{1.96\sqrt{(p)(1-p)}}{h} \right)^2$$

$$n = \left(\frac{1.96\sqrt{(0.5)(1-0.5)}}{.03} \right)^2$$

$n = 1{,}067.1$

In this case, with a $p = 0.5$, we would need to poll 1,068 (rounding up) people to be within 3 percent in estimating the chance of the candidate's being elected.

As you can see, the sample size of 683, with $p = 0.2$, is quite a bit less than the 1,068 required with $p = 0.5$. Since earlier polls may no longer be valid, most pollsters use the

1,068 as a standard. Using this formula, we have verified the pollsters requiring over 1,000 inputs on a close election to be within 3 percent on forecasting the election outcome with 95 percent confidence.

Equally, because the forecast has only 95 percent confidence, the prediction can be wrong 5 percent of the time!

In some cases we have a choice of getting variables or attribute data. Many companies choose to use go/no-go gauges for checking parts. This choice is made because go/no-go gauges are often easier to use than a variables gauge that gives measurement data. However, a go/no-go gauge checks only whether a part is within tolerance, either good or bad, and gives no indication as to *how* good or *how* bad a part is. This generates attribute data that are then used to calculate proportions.

Any process improvement with proportions is far more difficult, because it requires much larger sample sizes than the variables data used in the examples in the previous section. Using a gauge that gives variables (measurement) data output is a better choice!

With proportional data, comparing samples or a sample versus the population involves comparing ratios normally stated as decimals. These comparisons can be expressed in units of defects per hundred or of any other criterion that is consistent with both the sample and population. Although these proportions can be stated as decimals, the individual inputs are still attributes.

FORMULA: Comparing a proportional sample with the population (95 percent confidence)

First, we must calculate a test value Z_t.

$$Z_t = \frac{|p - P|}{\sqrt{\dfrac{P(1 - P)}{n}}}$$

P = proportion of defects (or whatever) in the population

p = proportion of defects (or same as above) in the sample

$|p - P|$ = absolute proportion difference (no minus sign in difference)

n = sample size

If Z_t is >1.96, then we can say with 95 percent confidence that the sample is statistically different from the population.

Following is the formula for comparing two proportional data samples to each other. We will then show a case study that incorporates the formulas for proportional data sample size, comparing a proportion sample with the population and comparing two proportion samples with each other.

FORMULA: Comparing two proportional data samples (95 percent confidence)

Calculate a test value Z_t.

$$Z_t = \frac{\left| \dfrac{x_1}{n_1} - \dfrac{x_2}{n_2} \right|}{\sqrt{\left(\dfrac{x_1 + x_2}{n_1 + n_2} \right)\left(1 - \dfrac{x_1 + x_2}{n_1 + n_2} \right)\left(\dfrac{1}{n_1} + \dfrac{1}{n_2} \right)}}$$

x_1 = number of defects (or whatever) in sample 1

x_2 = number of defects (or same as above) in sample 2

$\left| \dfrac{x_1}{n_1} - \dfrac{x_2}{n_2} \right|$ = absolute proportion difference (no minus sign in difference)

n_1 = size of sample 1

n_2 = size of sample 2

If Z_t is >1.96, then we can say with 95 percent confidence that the two samples are significantly different.

Case Study: Source of Crack

Glass lenses were automatically packed by a machine. The lenses were then shipped to another plant where they were assembled into a final consumer product. The customer's assembly machine would jam if a lens broke. During assembly 0.1 percent of the lenses were breaking, which caused excessive downtime. The assembly plant suspected that the lenses were being cracked during the automatic packing process at the lens plant and that these cracks would then break during assembly.

In order to test this theory, a test would be run where half the lenses would be randomly packed manually while the other half was being packed automatically. This randomness would make the lens population the same in both groups of packed lenses.

They decided to use a test sensitivity of 50 percent for the difference between the two samples because they believed that the automatic packer was the dominant source of the cracks and that the difference between the two packed samples would be dramatic. Even with this sensitivity, the calculated minimum sample size was 15,352 manually packed lenses!

The tests were run, with 15,500 lenses being manually packed and 15,500 lenses being auto packed.

The results were that 12 of the automatically packed components and 4 of the manually packed components broke when assembled. It was determined that this difference was statistically significant. Because of the costs involved in rebuilding the packer, they reran the test, and the results were similar.

The automatic packer was rebuilt, and the problem of the lenses' breaking in the assembly operation was no longer an issue.

Since the above case study incorporates all of the formulas we have covered in the use of samples on proportion data, we will use a series of problems to review in detail how the case study decisions were reached.

PROBLEM 9

Assuming we wish to be able to sense a 50 percent defect difference between two proportional data samples, and the historical defect level is 0.1 percent, what is the minimum number of samples we must study? Assume 95 percent confidence.

$p = 0.001$

$h = 0.0005$ (which is 50 percent of p)

$$n = \left(\frac{1.96\sqrt{(p)(1-p)}}{h} \right)^2$$

$$n = \left(\frac{1.96\sqrt{(0.001)(1-0.001)}}{0.0005} \right)^2$$

$n = 15{,}352$ (round up)

Answer: We would have to check at least 15,352 components to have 95 percent confidence that we could see a change of 0.05 percent. We decide to check 15,500 components.

PROBLEM 10

Of 15,500 automatically packed lenses, 12 broke during assembly. Of 15,500 manually packed lenses, 4 broke during assembly. Is the manually packed sample breakage statistically significantly different from the breakage in the auto packed sample?

$x_1 = 12$

$x_2 = 4$

$n_1 = 15{,}500$

$n_2 = 15{,}500$

$$Z_t = \frac{\left| \dfrac{x_1}{n_1} - \dfrac{x_2}{n_2} \right|}{\sqrt{\left(\dfrac{x_1 + x_2}{n_1 + n_2} \right)\left(1 - \dfrac{x_1 + x_2}{n_1 + n_2} \right)\left(\dfrac{1}{n_1} + \dfrac{1}{n_2} \right)}}$$

$$Z_t = \frac{\left| \dfrac{12}{15500} - \dfrac{4}{15500} \right|}{\sqrt{\left(\dfrac{12+4}{15500+15500} \right)\left(1 - \dfrac{12+4}{15500+15500} \right)\left(\dfrac{1}{15500} + \dfrac{1}{15500} \right)}}$$

$Z_t = 2.001$

Answer: Since 2.001 is greater than the test value of 1.96, we can say with 95 percent confidence that the manual pack test sample is significantly different than the baseline sample.

Because of the cost of rebuilding the packer, the test was rerun with similar results. The decision was then made to rebuild the packer.

In the previous section, we indicated that numerical data cannot be analyzed as variables if the discrimination is such that there are less than 10 steps within the range of interest. In Chapter 5, one of the example data sets had ages in whole years for a five-year period. Let's do a problem assuming we had such a data set, analyzing it as proportional data.

PROBLEM 11

A health study was being done on a group of men aged 50 to 55. Each man in the study had filled out a questionnaire related to his health. The men gave their ages in whole years. One of the questions on the questionnaire was whether they had seen a doctor within the previous year.

One element of the study was to ascertain whether the men in the study who were 55 years of age had seen a doctor in the last year more often than the others in the study. The people doing the study want to be able to sense a difference of 3 percent at a 95 percent confidence level.

This problem will involve comparing two proportions: the proportion of 55-year-old men who had seen a doctor in the last year and the proportion of 50- through 54-year-old men who have seen a doctor in the last year.

Since the number of men in the age 50- through 54-year-old group is much larger than the age 55 group, we will use that larger group as a population. (Note that this problem could also have been solved as a comparison between two samples.)

We first determine the minimum sample size.

$p = 0.5$ (The probability of having seen a doctor within the last year. Without additional information, this is the most conservative.)

$h = 0.03$

$$n = \left(\frac{1.96\sqrt{(p)(1-p)}}{h} \right)^2$$

$$n = \left(\frac{1.96\sqrt{(0.5)(1-0.5)}}{.03} \right)^2$$

$n = 1{,}067.1$

So the study must have at least 1,068 (rounding up) men 55 years of age.

Assume that the study had 1,500 men 55 years of age, which is more than the 1,068 minimum. There were 5,000 men aged 50 through 54. The questionnaire indicated that 828 of the men aged 55 had seen a doctor in the last year and 2,650 of the men aged 50 through 54 had seen a doctor.

$$Z_t = \frac{|p - P|}{\sqrt{\dfrac{P(1-P)}{n}}}$$

$P = 2650/5000 = 0.5300$ (Proportion of the study population aged 50 through 54 who had seen a doctor in the prior year)

$p = 828/1500 = 0.5520$ (Proportion in the age 55 group who had seen a doctor in the prior year)

$|p - P| = 0.02200$

$n = 1500$

$Z_t = 0.02200/0.01289$

$Z_t = 1.707$

Since 1.707 is not greater than 1.96, we can't say with 95 percent confidence that the men aged 55 saw a doctor in the last year at a higher rate than the men aged 50 through 54.

TESTING FOR STATISTICALLY SIGNIFICANT CHANGE, NONNORMAL DISTRIBUTIONS

What we will learn in this section is that many distributions are nonnormal and they occur in many places. But we can use the formulas and tables we have already reviewed to get meaningful information on any changes in the processes that generated these distributions. We often conduct Six Sigma work on nonnormal processes. Here are some examples:

Manufacturing

Any process having a zero at one end of the data is likely to have a skewed distribution. An example would be data representing distortion on a product.

Sales

If your salespeople tend to be made up of two distinct groups, one group experienced and the other inexperienced, the data distribution showing sales versus experience is likely to be bimodal.

Marketing

The data showing dollars spent in different markets may be nonnormal because of a focus on specific markets.

Accounting and Software Development

Error rate data may be strongly skewed based on the complexity or uniqueness of a program or accounting procedure.

Receivables

Delinquent receivables may be skewed based on the product or service involved.

Insurance

Costs at treatment centers in different cities may be nonnormal because of varying labor rates.

In the real world, nonnormal distributions are commonplace. Figure 8-6 gives some examples. Note that the plots in the figure are of the individual parts measurements.

Following are some examples of where these distributions would occur:

- The *uniform distribution* would occur if you plotted the numbers occurring on a spinning roulette wheel or from rolling a single die.
- The *skewed distribution* would be typical of a one-sided process, such as nonflatness on a machined part. Zero may be one end of the chart.
- The *bimodal distribution* can occur when there is play in a piece of equipment, where a process has a self-correcting feedback loop, or where there are two independent processes involved.

If the population is not normal, then the "absolute" probabilities generated from using computer programs or from tables may be somewhat in error. If we want to have good estimates of *absolute* probabilities from any computer program or table based on a normal distribution, the population must be normal.

However, since most of the work we do in Six Sigma involves *comparing similar processes relatively* (before and

FIGURE 8-6

Nonnormal distribution examples.
From Warren Brussee, *All About Six Sigma.*

| Uniform Distribution | Skewed Distribution | Bimodal Distribution |

after or between two similar processes) to see if we have made a significant change, these *relative* comparisons are valid even if the data we are using are nonnormal.

There are esoteric statistics based on nonnormal distributions and software packages that will give more accurate estimates of actual probabilities, but they require someone very knowledgeable in statistics. This added degree of accuracy is not required for most Six Sigma work, where we are looking for significant change and not absolute values.

TIP
Statistical tests on variables, nonnormal data

You can use the statistical tests in this book for evaluating change, including referencing the numbers in the standardized normal distribution table (Figure 7-6), to compare a process before and after a change, or to compare processes with similarly shaped nonnormal distributions. However, although the relative qualitative comparison is valid, the absolute probability values on each process may be somewhat inaccurate.

As in checking processes with normal distributions, the distributions that are nonnormal must be periodically plotted to verify that the shapes of the distributions are still similar. If a distribution shape has changed dramatically, you cannot use the formulas or charts in this book for before and after comparisons. However, similar processes usually have and keep similarly shaped distributions.

WHAT WE HAVE LEARNED IN CHAPTER 8

- Valid sampling and analysis of variables data are needed for the Define, Measurement, Analysis, and Control steps in the DMAIC process.
- The rule-of-thumb minimum sample size on variables data is 11. When possible use the formulas to determine minimum sample size.
- We seldom have complete data on a population, but use samples to estimate its composition.
- We normally work to a 95 percent confidence test level.

- Assume two-tailed (high *and* low) problems unless specifically indicated as one-tailed.
- We normally want to sense a change equal to 10 percent of the tolerance, or $0.6S$.
- When checking for a change, we can compare a sample with earlier population data or compare two samples with each other.
- We follow a three-step process when analyzing for change. Compare distribution shapes first, then sigma, and then averages. If significant change is identified at any step in the process, we stop. We then must decide what to do with the knowledge that the process changed.
- Proportional data is generated from attribute inputs such as yes and no and go and no-go. Testing for statistically significant change with proportional data involves comparing proportions, or ratios, stated as decimals.
- Proportional data requires much larger sample sizes than variables data.
- We generally want to be able to sense a change of 10 percent of the difference between the proportions or 10 percent of the tolerance.
- We often do Six Sigma work on nonnormal processes. You can use the included statistical tests for calculating differences on similarly shaped nonnormal distributions.
- On nonnormal distributions, the absolute probability values obtained may be somewhat inaccurate. But comparing probabilities to determine qualitative change on a process or on similar processes is valid.

PART FIVE

Process Control, DOEs, and RSS Tolerances

General and Focused Control

GENERAL PROCESS CONTROL

In this chapter we discuss different ways to keep a process in control and the related challenges. This relates to the Control step in the DMAIC process.

The earlier chapters discussed the means of improving a process or product. However, some improvements are eventually forgotten or ignored, and the process is put back to the way it was before the change. To avoid backsliding, process control is essential.

It is impossible to make an all-inclusive list on control details, since they vary so much per project or process need. However, here are some general guidelines:

- Communication on change detail and the rationale for the range is critical on *every* change. This communication must include instructions for changing any tolerance, procedure, or data sheet related to the change. Instructions should be given to scrap old drawings or instructions, and feedback must give assurance that this was done.

- When possible, make a quantitative physical change that is obvious to all, with enough of a change that the new part is obviously different. Destroy, or make

inaccessible, all previous equipment that doesn't
include the change.

- If the change is qualitative, then make sure appropriate
  training, quality checks, gauges and verifications, and
  operator feedback are in place.
- For some period of time after the change is
  implemented, periodically verify that the expected
  gains are truly occurring.

As companies downsize and people are reduced, control
becomes an even bigger challenge. As mentioned earlier, the
best Six Sigma solutions relate to mechanical changes to a process, with little reliance on people's actions to maintain a gain.

TRADITIONAL CONTROL CHARTS

Traditional control charts have two graphs. The top graph is
based on the process average, with statistically based control
rules and limits telling the operator when the process is in or
out of control. This graph cannot have any reference to the
product tolerance because it is displaying product averages.
A tolerance is for individual parts and is meaningless when
used on averages.

The second graph on a traditional control chart is based on
the process variation (or sigma), also with rules and limits.

If either of these graphs shows an out-of-control situation, the operator is supposed to work on the process.
However, the charts are somewhat confusing to operators.
Sometimes the control chart will show an out-of-control situation while quality checks do not show product out of specification. Also, one graph can show the process as in control
while the other shows it out of control.

SIMPLIFIED CONTROL CHARTS

This tool is primarily for those involved in manufacturing or
process work and is used in the Control step of the DMAIC
process.

Control charts have a chaotic history. In the 1960s, when Japan was showing the United States what quality really meant, the United States tried to implement some quick fixes, which included control charts. Few understood control charts, and they were never used enough to realize their full potential. However, simplified control charts, as described in this section, have had some impressive successes.

In most cases, the customer will be happy with the product if a supplier can reduce defect excursions (incidence of higher-than-normal quality issues). This does not necessarily mean that all products are within specification. It means that the customer has designed his or her process to work with the normal incoming product. So, the emphasis should be on reducing defect excursions, which is the reason control charts were designed.

A single chart, as used on the simplified control chart, can give the operator process feedback in a format that is understandable and intuitive. It is intuitive because it shows the average and the predicted data spread on one bar. This is the way an operator thinks of his or her process.

Assume that the operator is regularly getting variables data on a critical dimension. Without regular variables data that are entered into some kind of computer or network, control charts are not effective. Refer to the simplified control chart in Figure 9-1 as the following is discussed.

Each vertical feedback bar that is displayed will be based on the data from the previous 11 product readings. The average $\bar{x}$ and sigma s will be calculated from these 11 readings. The displayed vertical bar will have a small horizontal dash representing the average $\bar{x}$, and the vertical bar will be ±-3 sigma in height from the horizontal average dash.

If the end of a vertical bar crosses a control limit, the vertical bar will be yellow. The control limit is midway between the specification and the historical three-sigma measurements based on data taken during a time period when the process was running well. A yellow bar (in Figure 9-1, these are vertical bars 15, 16, 22, and 23 counting from the left side

FIGURE 9–1

Simplified control chart.
From Warren Brussee, *All About Six Sigma.*

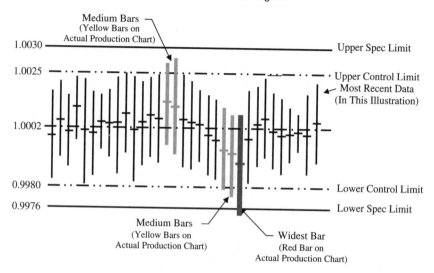

of the graph) is the trigger for the operator to review and/or adjust the process.

If the vertical bar crosses a specification limit, the vertical bar will be red (in Figure 9-1, this is vertical bar 24 counting from the left side of the graph). This communicates to the operator that some of the product are predicted to be out of specification. Setting up the type of graph shown in Figure 9-1 will require some computer skills.

A tolerance limit can be shown on this chart because the individual part's projected ±3 sigma measurement spread is represented by each vertical line. This is equivalent to having individual data points displayed. However, a control limit is also displayed on this chart, to which the operator has to learn to respond. This quicker reaction often saves work, because it will require only process "tweaks" rather than major process changes.

An operator using this kind of control chart will quickly learn that he or she can see trends in either the average or variation and use that information to help in the debugging of the process. The information is intuit and requires little training.

> **TIP**
> Use simplified control charts on equipment or process output
>
> Any piece of equipment or process that makes product that is generally acceptable to the customer, with the exception of defect excursions, is a natural for simplified control charts.

Although the most common benefit derived from the simplified control chart is reduced defect excursions, it also helps drive process insights and breakthroughs.

WHAT WE HAVE LEARNED IN CHAPTER 9

- Communication on the change reason and rationale is critical on *every* change.
- When possible, make a quantitative physical change that is obvious to all.
- If the change is qualitative, make sure appropriate training, quality checks, gauges and verifications, and operator feedback are in place.
- Simplified control charts give the operator process feedback in a format that is understandable, intuit, and encourages reaction before product is out of specification.
- Tolerances can be shown on a simplified control chart, whereas they cannot be displayed on a traditional control chart.

Design of Experiments and Tolerance Analysis

DESIGN OF EXPERIMENTS

Design of experiments is not an area in which green belts are normally expected to have expertise. But it is important that they be aware of this tool and its use.

In an optimized process, all the inputs are at settings that give the best and most stable output. To determine these optimum settings, all key process input variables (KPIVs) must be run at various levels with the results then analyzed to identify which settings give the best results. The methodology to perform this optimization is called *design of experiments* (DOEs.)

This section applies to the Improve step in the DMAIC process, and it is primarily for those involved in manufacturing or process work. A DOE is usually conducted right in the production environment using the actual production equipment.

Here are some of the challenges of running a DOE:

- It is difficult to identify a limited list of KPIVs to test.
- It is difficult to keep in control the variables *not* being tested.

- A large number of test variables require many trial iterations and setups.
- The results of the DOE must then be tested under controlled conditions.
- What to use as an output goal is not a trivial concern.

A *simplified* DOE, as described in this book, will minimize these difficulties.

NOTE

The final results of a DOE are usually *not* the keys that drive process improvement. It is the disciplined process of setting up and running the test and the insights gleaned during the test that drive improvement.

SIMPLIFIED DOEs

Here are the steps to run an effective simplified DOE.

1. Develop a list of key process input variables and prioritize them.
2. Test combinations of variables. To test two variables A and B, each at two values 1 and 2, there are four possible combinations: A1/B1, A2/B1, A1/B2, and A2/B2. To test three variables, each at two values, there are eight combinations: A1/B1/C1, A2/B1/C1, A1/B2/C1, A1/B1/C2, A2/B2/C1, A2/B1/C2, A1/B2/C2, and A2/B2/C2.

Each of the above combinations should be run a *minimum* of five times. This means that a test of two variables should have a minimum of $4 \times 5 = 20$ setups and a test of three variables should have a minimum of $8 \times 5 = 40$ setups.

Do each setup independently of the earlier one. Also, each setup should be in random order.

Below are the typical results you may see from running a DOE on two variables each at two different settings. We have calculated the average and sigma for each combination.

Group	A1/B1	A2/B1	A1/B2	A2/B2
Delta average from nominal (in inches)	0.00023	0.00009	0.00037	0.00020
Sigma on readings (in inches)	0.00093	0.00028	0.00092	0.00033

The results show that A2/B1 had the closest average to the nominal diameter, being off only 0.00009 inch. This group also had the lowest sigma at 0.00028 inch. We would use our earlier statistics to test if this group is statistically different than the next nearest group. If it is, then we would do a controlled run to verify that the results can be duplicated.

If one group had the closest average, but a different group had a lower sigma, we would normally go with the lower sigma since the process center (average) can often be adjusted easily.

RSS TOLERANCES

Root-sum-of-squares (RSS) tolerance stack-up is normally considered part of design for Six Sigma, and green belts aren't expected to have expertise in this area. But the issue of tolerances comes up so often that it is wise for green belts to have some awareness of this process.

Stacked parts are akin to having multiple blocks with each block placed on top of another. When multiple parts are stacked and they have cumulative tolerance buildup, the traditional way to handle the stack-up variation was to assume the worst case on each component.

Example: Assume there is a stack of 9 blocks, each a nominal 1.000-inch thick, and the tolerance on each part is ±0.003 inch. A traditional worst-case design would assume the following:

Maximum stack height = 1.003 inches * 9 = 9.027 inches
Minimum stack height = 0.997 inches * 9 = 8.973 inches

The problem with this analysis is that the odds of *all* the parts being at the maximum or *all* the parts being at the minimum are extremely low. Hence the use of the RSS approach.

The RSS Approach to Calculating Tolerances

Using the RSS approach on our example, let's calculate what the tolerance should be on the stack of blocks if we assume that ±3 sigma (6s or 99.73 percent) of the products are within the 0.006-inch tolerance. So:

$$6s = 0.006 \text{ inch (the tolerance)}$$
$$s = 0.001 \text{ inch}$$

The formula to solve for the sigma S of the total stack is

$$S = \sqrt{n(1.3s)^2}$$

In this case, $n = 9$ (number of blocks), $s = 0.001$ inch. So $S = 0.0039$ inch.

Assuming the stack specification is set at ±3 sigma, we then have

Maximum stack height = $9 + 3S = 9.012$ inches

Minimum stack height = $9 - 3S = 8.988$ inches

As you can see, the RSS method resulted in a far tighter tolerance for the stack of parts. The example showed parts of equal thicknesses, but the same concept can be used on parts of varying thicknesses.

WHAT WE HAVE LEARNED IN CHAPTER 10

- Design of Experiments (DOEs) attempt to optimize a process, such that all KIPVs are at settings that give the best, most stable output.
- The process of running a disciplined DOE is what often gives the most valuable insights.
- RSS tolerance calculations are generally more reality based than assuming the worst possible stack-up dimensions.

The Six Sigma Statistical Tool Finder Matrix

Look in the Need and Detail columns in the matrix below to identify the appropriate Six Sigma tool.

Need	Detail	Six Sigma Tool	Location
Address customer needs by identifying and prioritizing actions	Convert qualitative customer input to specific prioritized actions.	Simplified QFDs	Chapter 3
Minimize collateral damage due to a product or process change	Convert qualitative input on concerns to specific prioritized actions.	Simplified FMEAs	Chapter 3
Identify key process input variables (KPIVs)	Use expert input on a process.	Cause-and-effect fishbone diagrams	Chapter 4
	Use historical data.	Correlation tests	
Pinpoint possible problem areas of a process	Use expert input.	Process flow diagrams	Chapter 4
Verify measurement accuracy	Determine if a gauge is adequate for the task.	Simplified gauge verifications	Chapter 6
Calculate minimum sample size	Variables (decimal) data	Sample size, variables	Chapter 8
	Proportional data	Sample size, proportions	

Need	Detail	Six Sigma Tool	Location
Determine if there has been a statistically significant change on variables (decimal) data	Compare a sample with population data. Compare two samples to each other.	(1) Plot data (2) Chi-square tests (3) t tests (1) Plot data (2) F tests (3) t tests	Chapter 8
Determine if there has been a statistically significant change on proportional data.	The mathematical probability of the population is known.	Excel's BINOMDIST	Chapter 7
	Compare a sample to a population where both proportions are calculated.	Sample/population formula	Chapter 8
Determine if tolerances are appropriate	How were tolerances determined?	Need-based tolerances	Chapter 10
	Are parts "stacked"?	RSS tolerances	
Control process	General guidelines	General process control	Chapter 9
	Variables data to operator	Simplified control charts	
Optimize process	Test inputs on production line.	Simplified DOEs	Chapter 10

GLOSSARY

Accuracy: A measurement concept involving the correctness of the average reading. It is the extent to which the average of the measurements taken agrees with a true value.

Analyze: The third step in the DMAIC problem-solving method. The measurements/data must be analyzed to see if they are consistent with the problem definition and also to identify a root cause. A problem solution is then identified.

Attributes: A qualitative characteristic that can be counted. Examples: good or bad, go or no-go, yes or no.

Black belt: A person who has Six Sigma training and skills sufficient to act as an instructor, mentor, and expert to green belts. This book does not require black belts.

Chi-square test: A test used on variables (decimal) data to see if there was a statistically significant change in the sigma between the population data and the current sample data.

Confidence tests between groups of data: Tests used to determine if there is a statistically significant change between samples or between a sample and a population.

Continuous data (variables data):   Data that can have any value in a continuum. Theoretically, they are decimal data without "steps."

Control: The final step in the DMAIC problem-solving method.

Correlation testing: A tool that uses historical data to find what variables changed at the same time or position as the problem time or position.

Cumulative: In probability problems, the sum of the probabilities of getting "the number of successes or less," like getting 3 *or less* heads on 5 flips of a coin. This option is used on "less-than" and "more-than" problems.

Define: This is the overall problem definition step in the DMAIC. This definition should be as specific as possible.

DMAIC (define, measure, analyze, improve, control) problem-solving method: The Six Sigma problem-solving approach used by green belts. This is the roadmap that is followed for all projects and process improvements.

Excel BINOMDIST: Not technically a Six Sigma tool, but the tool recommended in this text for determining the probability that observed proportional data are the result of purely random causes. This tool is used when we already know the mathematical probability of a population event.

F test: A test used on variables (decimal) data to see if there was a statistically significant change in the sigma between two samples.

Fishbone diagram: A Six Sigma tool that uses a representation of a fish skeleton to help trigger identification of all the variables that can be contributing to a problem. The problem is shown as the fish head. The variables are shown on the bones.

Green belt: The primary implementer of the Six Sigma methodology. He or she has competence on all the primary Six Sigma tools.

Improve: The fourth step in the DMAIC problem-solving method. Once a solution has been analyzed, the fix must be implemented.

Labeling averages and standard deviations: We label the average of a population $\overline{X}$ and the sample average $\overline{x}$. Similarly, the standard deviation (sigma) of the population is labeled S and the sample standard deviation (sigma) is labeled s.

Lean Six Sigma: A methodology to reduce manufacturing costs by reducing lead time, reducing work-in-process, minimizing wasted motion, optimizing work area design, and streamlining material flow.

Master black belt: A person who has management responsibility for a separate Six Sigma organization. This book does not require master black belts.

Measure: The second step of the DMAIC problem-solving method.

Minimum sample size: The number of data points needed to enable statistically valid comparisons or predictions.

n: The sample size or, in probability problems, the number of independent trials, like the number of coin tosses or the number of parts measured.

Need-based tolerance: A Six Sigma tool that emphasizes that often tolerances are not established based on the customer's real need, and tolerances should therefore be reviewed periodically.

Normal distribution: A bell-shaped distribution of data that is indicative of the distribution of data from many things in nature. Information on this type of distribution is used to predict populations based on samples of data.

Number s (or x successes):   The total number of successes that you are looking for in a probability problem, like getting exactly three heads. This is used in the Excel BINOMDIST program.

Plot data: Data plotted on a graph. Most processes with variables data have data plot shapes that stay consistent unless a major change to the process has occurred. If the shapes of the data plots have changed dramatically, then the quantitative formulas cannot be used to compare the processes.
Probability: The likelihood of an event happening by pure chance.
Probability *p* (or probability *s*):   The probability of a success on each individual trial, like the likelihood of a head on one coin flip or a defect on one part. This is always a proportion and generally stated as a decimal, like 0.0156.
Probability *P*:   In Excel's BINOMDIST, the probability of getting a given number of successes from all the trials, like a certain number of heads in a number of coin tosses, or a given number of defects in a shipment of parts.
Process flow diagram: A type of flow chart that gives specific locations or times of process events.
Proportional data: Data based on attribute inputs, such as good or bad, or stepped numerical data.

Repeatability: The consistency of measurements obtained when one person measures a part multiple times with the same device.
Reproducibility: The consistency of measurements obtained when two or more people measure a part multiple times with the same device.

Sample size, proportional data: A tool used for calculating the minimum sample size needed to get representative attribute data on a process generating proportional data.
Sample size, variables data: A tool used for calculating the minimum sample size needed to get representative data on a process with variables (decimal) data.
Simplified DOE (design of experiment):   A Six Sigma tool that enables tests to be made on an existing process to establish optimum settings on the key process input variables (KPIVs).
Simplified FMEA (failure mode and effects analysis):   A Six Sigma tool used to convert qualitative concerns on collateral damage to a prioritized action plan.
Simplified gauge verification: A Six Sigma tool used on variables data (decimals) to verify that the gauge is capable of giving the required accuracy of measurements compared to the allowable tolerance.
Simplified QFD (quality function deployment):   A Six Sigma tool used to convert qualitative customer input into specific prioritized action plans.
Six Sigma methodology: A specific problem-solving approach that uses Six Sigma tools to improve processes and products. This methodology is data driven, and the goal is to reduce unacceptable products or events.

T test: A Six Sigma test used on variables data to see if there is a statistically significant change in the average between population data and the current sample data, or between two samples.

Variables data: Continuous data that are generally in decimal form. Theoretically you could look at enough decimal places to find that no two values are exactly the same.

RELATED READING

Berk, Kenneth N., and Patrick Carey. *Data Analysis with Microsoft Excel*. (Southbank, Australia, and Belmont, Calif.: Brooks/Cole, 2004.)

Brussee, Warren T. *All About Six Sigma*. (New York: McGraw-Hill, 2006.)

Brussee, Warren T. *Statistics for Six Sigma Made Easy*. (New York: McGraw-Hill, 2004.)

Capinski, Marek, and Tomasz Zastawniak. *Probability Through Problems*. (New York: Springer-Verlag, 2001.)

Cohen, Louis. *Quality Function Deployment: How to Make QFD Work for You*. (Upper Saddle River, N.J.: Prentice-Hall PTR, 1995.)

Harry, Mikel J., and Richard Schroeder. *Six Sigma: The Breakthrough Management Strategy/Revolutionizing the World's Top Organizations*. (New York: Random House/Doubleday/Currency, 1999.)

Harry, Mikel J., and Reigle Stewart. *Six Sigma Mechanical Design Tolerancing*, 2nd ed. (Scaumburg, Ill.: Motorola University Press, 1988.)

Hoerl, Roger W., and Ronald D. Snee. *Statistical Thinking: Improving Business Performance*. (Pacific Grove, Calif.: Duxbury-Thompson Learning, 2002.)

Jaisingh, Lloyd R. *Statistics for the Utterly Confused*. (New York: McGraw-Hill, 2000.)

Kiemele, Mark J., Stephen R. Schmidt, and Ronald J. Berdine. *Basic Statistics, Tools for Continuous Improvement*, 4th ed. (Colorado Springs, Colo.: Air Academy Press, 1997.)

Levine, David M., and David Stephan, Timothy C. Krehbiel, and Mark L. Berenson. *Statistics for Managers, Using Microsoft Excel (with CD-ROM)*, 4th ed. (Upper Saddle River, N.J.: Prentice-Hall 2004.)

McDermott, Robin E., Raymond J. Mikulak, and Michael R. Beauregard. *The Basics of FMEA*. (New York: Quality Resources, 1996.)

Mizuno, Shigeru, and Yoji Akao, editors. *QFD: The Customer-Driven Approach to Quality Planning and Deployment*. (Tokyo: Asian Productivity Organization, 1994.)

Montgomery, Douglas C. *Design and Analysis of Experiments*, 5th ed. (New York: Wiley, 2001.)

Pande, Peter S., Robert P. Neuman, and Roland R. Cavanagh. *The Six Sigma Way: How GE, Motorola, and Other Top Companies are Honing Their Performance*. (New York: McGraw-Hill, 2000.)

Pyzdek, Thomas. *The Six Sigma Handbook, Revised and Expanded: The Complete Guide for Greenbelts, Blackbelts, and Managers at All Levels.* (New York: McGraw-Hill, 2003.)

Rath & Strong Management Consultants. *Rath & Strong's Six Sigma Pocket Guide.* (New York: McGraw-Hill, 2003.)

Schmidt, Stephen R., and Robert G. Launsby. *Understanding Industrial Designed Experiments* (with CD-ROM), 4th ed. (Colorado Springs, Colo.: Air Academy Press, 1997.)

Smith, Dick, and Jerry Blakeslee. *Strategic Six Sigma: Best Practices from the Executive Suite.* (Hoboken, N.J.: Wiley, 2002.)

Stamatis, D. H. *Failure Mode and Effect Analysis: FMEA from Theory to Execution,* 2nd ed. (Milwaukee: American Society for Quality, 2003.)

Swinscow, T. D. V., and M. J. Cambell. *Statistics at Square One,* 10th ed. (London: BMJ Books, 2001.)

INDEX

Accounting
    fishbone diagrams for, 32
    histograms for, 93
    nonnormal distributions for, 151
    probability in, 84
    proportional data for, 141
    simplified FMEA for, 24
    simplified process flow diagrams
        for, 35
    simplified QFD for, 17
    time plots for, 41
    variables data for, 116
Accuracy
    defining, 73, 169
    of numbers, 53
    of Z value, 107
Agency for Healthcare Research and
    Quality, 4
Aim. *See* Accuracy
Analysis, 53. *See also* Regression
    analysis
    of data, 3, 11, 124
    long-term drift confusing, 61
    regression, 40
    statistical, 50, 108
Attribute data, 51, 169
    analyzed as proportional data, 53
    variables data v., 144
Attribute inputs, 141
Average
    change in, 107
    checking, 129–133, 137–139
    labeling, 118, 170
    movement of, 66
    nominal target differing from, 58
    in numerator, 119
    process, 158

Bimodal data
    distribution of, 150–151
    shape of, 103
Bin edge
    specific, 111
    value of, in histogram, 94
BINOMDIST, 85–92, 169
Bins per histogram, 113
Black belt, 169–170

Cause and effect, 44
Centering, 66–67, 94
Chi-square test, 139, 169. *See also*
    Simplified chi-square
    distribution table
    Sigma change detected by,
        128–129
Collection
    of data, 53, 68
    of samples, 53–55
Communication
    on change, 157
    openness of, 40
Competition, 24
Computers, 99. *See also* Software
    development
    blind use of, 108
    doing plotted Data, 108–113
    forms on, 21
    probability from, 107
    traditional process flow diagram
        on, 37
Confidence
    95%, 122, 124, 146
    tests of, 139
Consumer input, 10
Continuous data. *See* Variables data

Control
 challenges of, 158
 of input variables, 65
 of quality, 11
 of samples, 68
Control charts
 simplified, 11, 158–161
 traditional, 158
Correlation tests, 169
 instructions for, 41–44
Cumulative, 85, 169
Customer. *See also* Voice of the
   customer
 cost v. needs of, 121
 defining, 17
 needs of, 15, 19, 121
 profits v., 24
 referring back to, 68
 satisfaction, 55

Data. *See also* Proportional data;
   Variables data
 adjustment of, 57
 analysis of, 3, 11, 124
 attribute, 51, 53, 144, 169
 bimodal, 103, 150–151
 collection, 53, 68
 comparative-effectiveness, 16
 discreet, 42
 discrimination, 50–53
 distribution of, 127
 ends of, 95
 error, 71
 gathering, 54–55
 historical, 42
 improvement shown by, 56
 measurement, 144
 nonsymmetrical, 103
 normal, 93
 normal curve standardized, 98
 numerical, 148
 outliers of, 126
 plots, 92–94
 plotted, 45, 103, 108–113, 171
 randomness of, 98–99
 stepped, 141

types of, 49–50
 variation of, 58
Defects, 90
 of 3 sigma process, 60–61
 cost of, 7
 excursion, 159
 per opportunity, 8
Defects per million (DPM), 7–8
Defects per million opportunities
   (DPMO), 7–8
Define, Measure, Analyze, Improve,
   Control (DMAIC)
 formulas for, 115
 green belts approach to, 8–11,
   169–170
 using, 11
Degrees of freedom, 139
Design item, 19–20
Design of experiments (DOE), 163–164
Designer's Dozen, 22
Discrimination, 148
Distribution, 92–93. *See also* Pro-
   cess distribution
 of bimodal data, 150–151
 checking, 125–128, 134
 shape of, 152
 uniform, 151
DMAIC. *See* Define, Measure,
   Analyze, Improve, Control
DOE. *See* Design of experiments
DPM. *See* Defects per million
DPMO. *See* Defects per million
   opportunities

Equipment
 simplified control charts for, 159
Error. *See also* Gauge error
 data, 71
 differentiating, 62
 incidence of, 84
 input variables affecting, 64
 measurement of, 72
 periodic, 67
 predominant, 75
 quantity, 8
 types of, 124

Estimation, 140
Excel
    BINOMDIST in, 85–92, 170
    graphing program of, 110–113
    histogram, 112
    normal distribution from, 107
    NORMSDIST in, 107
Experts, 33

F test, 134–135, 139, 170. *See also*
    Simplified F table
Failure modes and effects analy-
    sis (FMEA), 23–25. *See also*
    Simplified FMEA; Traditional
    FMEA
Feedback, 159, 161
Fishbone diagrams, 170
    brainstorming assisted, 20
    detail of, 68–69
    input variables in, 67
    instructions for, 32–34
    population identified with, 63–64
    process control diagram used
        with, 34
    purpose of, 31–32
FMEA. *See* Failure modes and ef-
    fects analysis
Forms
    complexity of, 23
    on computers, 21
    QFD, 21–22
    simplified FMEA, 25–28
    simplified QFD, 18–19

Gauge error
    acceptable, 78
    calculating, 77
    checking for, 73–74
    maximum, 72
    simplified gauge verification for,
        71–72
Gauge reading, 72
Gauge R&R, 78–79
General Electric, 4–5
General process control guidelines,
    157–158

Go/no-go gauges, 53, 144
Graphing programs
    complexity of, 109
    Excel's, 110–113
Green belts, 5–6
    DMAIC approach by, 8–11,
        169–170
    expertise of, 165

Hawthorne effect, 55–56
Histogram, 128
    bin edge value in, 94
    bins per, 113
    Excel, 112
    on processes, 93
    shape of, 97

Independence, 96
Independent trials, 88
Input variables. *See also* Attribute
        inputs; Key process input
        variables
    categories of, 33
    control of, 65
    correlations with, 42
    errors affected by, 64
    in fishbone diagram, 67
Inspection, 57
Insurance
    data for, 55
    fishbone diagrams for, 32
    histograms for, 94
    nonnormal distributions for, 151
    probability in, 84
    proportional data for, 141
    simplified FMEA for, 24–25
    simplified process flow diagrams
        for, 35
    simplified QFD for, 17
    time plots for, 41
    variables data for, 116

Key process input variables (KPIV),
    31
    changing, 41–42
    expert-picked, 64–65

Key process input variables (*Cont.*)
  prioritizing, 164
  probable causes identified by, 32
  problem affecting, 35
  simple, 43
KPIV. *See* Key Process input variables

Lean manufacturing
  Toyota starting, 35
  from traditional Six Sigma, 5
Lean Six Sigma, 5
  areas of, 34
  conflict minimized during, 40
  methodology of, 170
  simplified process flow diagram
    for, 37
  VOC referred by, 15
Long-term drift
  analysis confused by, 61
  expected, 108

Management
  commitment of, 5
  scientific, 39
Manufacturing. *See also* Lean man-
    ufacturing
  fishbone diagrams for, 32
  histograms for, 93
  nonnormal distributions for, 150
  probability in, 83
  proportional data for, 140
  samples and, 54
  simplified control charts for, 158
  simplified FMEA for, 23–24
  simplified process flow diagrams
    for, 35
  simplified QFD for, 16
  time plots for, 41
  variables data for, 115
Marketing
  data for, 54
  fishbone diagrams for, 32
  histograms for, 93
  nonnormal distributions for, 150
  probability in, 84

proportional data for, 141
simplified FMEA for, 24
simplified process flow diagrams
  for, 35
simplified QFD for, 16–17
time plots for, 41
variables data for, 116
Master black belt, 170
Masters
  random, 74–75
  for simplified gauge verification, 74
  specification of, 75
Materials, 39
Matrix of Matrices, 22
Measurement
  consistency of, 171
  data, 144
  error in, 72
  plotting, 125, 134
  problem process, 10
  of process, 54–55
  of productivity, 56
  spread of, 62
  steps of, 52
  variables data, 50
Methodology
  of lean Six Sigma, 170
  of Motorola, 4
  numerical, 42
  quantitative, 125
  Six Sigma, 171
Metrics, 7–8
Motorola
  1.5 sigma process drift of, 108
  methodology of, 4
  process drift assumed by, 61

N, 85, 170
Need-based Tolerance, 170
Nonnormal distributions, 150–152
Nonsymmetrical data, 103
Normal curve standardized data, 98
Normal data, 93, 108–109
Normal distribution, 93, 102, 103.
  See also Standardized normal
  distribution table

curve of, 97
from Excel, 107
shape of, 170
specifying, 98
symmetry of, 103
Normal process
samples of, 63
standardized normal distribution
use on, 99
NORMSDIST, 107
Null hypothesis, 139
Numbers s, 85, 170

Off-center process, 63–66
One-tailed problem, 123
Operator
process feedback to, 159
trends spotted by, 160
Opportunity, 8
Outliers, 125

Performance
metrics gauging, 7–8
poor, 91–92
testing for, 122–123
Plots
data, 92–94
time, 41, 43–44
Plotted Data, 171
computers doing, 108–113
correlations on, 45
normal distribution using, 103
Population
estimating, 119–120
fishbone diagram identifying,
63–64
nonnormal, 151
of process, 54
proportional sample v., 144–145
sample v., 118, 124
sigma, 132
uniformity of, 55
Predictions, 54
Probability, 49
absolute, 152
from computers, 107

cumulative, 86
definition of, 171
establishing, 83–84
techniques, 96–97
updating, 143
uses of, 84–92
Z value related to, 121
Probability P, 85, 171
Probability p, 85, 171
Problem process, 10
Problems
defining of, 9–10
dimension related, 63
identification of, 31
of interest, 32
KPIV affecting, 35
one-tailed, 123
sampling, 55
simplified process flow diagrams
identifying, 34–36
solving, 7–9
specification of, 66–67
two-tailed, 121
unexpected, 24
Process
average, 158
centering of, 66–67, 94
change, 107, 131
comparison between, 127, 133
control diagram, 34
debug, 36
distribution, 125, 128, 134
drift, 61, 108
flow charts, 39
flow diagram, 171
histogram on, 93
improving, 11, 144
mean of, 107
measurement of, 10, 54–55
modifications, 20
off-center, 63–66
operator feedback on, 159
optimized, 163
population of, 54
sigma level, 7–8, 59–60
stability of, 119

Process (*Cont.*)
  standardized normal distribution
    table to compare, 152
  3 sigma, 60–61
  variation in, 59, 62, 67–69, 158
Process distribution
  over time, 125, 134
  qualitative change in, 128
Process sigma level
  DPM enabled by, 7–8
  equations, 59–60
Process variation
  sigma related to, 59
  tolerance compared to, 62
  traditional control charts based
    on, 158
Product development, 16
Productivity measurement, 56
Project input, 25
Proportional data, 49–50
  attribute data analyzed as, 53
  comparison of, 148
  sample size and, 142–144, 171
  statistical significance using,
    140–142
  variables data *vs.*, 141
Proportional sample
  comparison between, 145
  population v., 144–145

QFD. *See* Quality function
    deployment
Quality control, 11
Quality function deployment (QFD).
    See also Simplified QFD;
    Traditional QFD
  form, 21–22
  four forms of, 21
  simplified QFD v., 15–17
Quality system, 117
Quantitative method, 126
Quantity error, 8
Queuing, 35

Random data, 98–99
Random results, 122–123

Rating
  of design item, 19–20
Ratios, 49
Receivables
  data for, 54–55
  fishbone diagrams for, 32
  histograms for, 93
  nonnormal distributions for, 151
  probability in, 84
  proportional data for, 141
  simplified process flow diagrams
    for, 35
  simplified QFD for, 17
  time plots for, 41
  variables data for, 116
Reference points, 96, 99
Regression analysis, 40
Repeatability, 73, 78–79, 171
Reproducibility, 73, 78–79, 171
Root-sum-of-squares (RSS), 165–166
RSS. *See* Root-sum-of-squares

Sales
  fishbone diagrams for, 32
  histograms for, 93
  nonnormal distributions for, 151
  probability in, 83–84
  proportional data for, 141
  sampling for, 54
  simplified FMEA for, 24
  simplified process flow diagrams
    for, 35
  simplified QFD for, 16–17
  time plots for, 41
  variables data for, 116
Sample sigmas, 119, 137
Sample size
  differences in, 119
  large, 141
  maximizing, 120
  minimum, 123, 132, 142,
    148–149, 170
  proportional data and, 142–144,
    171
  of quality system, 117
  on variables data, 120–124, 171

Samples. *See also* Proportional
    sample
  change between, 133–139
  collection of, 53–55
  comparing, 115–116
  control of, 68
  difficulties regarding, 57
  multiple, 119–120
  of normal process, 63
  population v., 117, 124
  problems with, 55
  random, 58
  of sigma, 118, 137
Scientific management, 39
Sensitivity
  calculating, 120–121, 142–144
  of results v. target, 123
  test, 146
Shape
  of bimodal data, 103
  of distribution, 152
  of histogram, 97
  of normal distribution, 170
Sigma, 158. *See also* Six Sigma
  calculating, 59–60
  checking, 128–129, 134
  chi-square test detecting change
    in, 128–129
  estimating, 109
  population, 132
  process variation related to, 59–60
  reduction of, 105, 107
  sample, 119, 137
  values, 97
  on variables, 117
Sigma level, 7–8, 59–60
Simplified chi-square distribution
    table, 130, 131
Simplified control charts, 11, 160
  for equipment, 159
  feedback from, 161
  for manufacturing, 158
Simplified DOE, 164–165, 171
Simplified F table, 135–137
Simplified FMEA, 171
  FMEA v., 23–25

forms, 25–28
  instructions for, 25–27
  simplified QFD done before, 27–28
  traditional FMEA v., 28
Simplified gauge verification
  components of, 73–74
  examples of, 76–79
  for gauge error, 71–72
  improvement from, 78
  instructions for, 74–76
  masters for, 74
  in Six Sigma, 72–73
  used on variables data, 171
Simplified process flow diagrams
  instructions for, 37–40
  problems identified by, 34–36
Simplified QFD, 171
  form, 18–19
  instructions for, 17–21
  QFD v., 15–17
  simplified FMEA done after,
    27–28
  traditional QFD v., 22–23
Simplified t distribution table, 132
  t-test compared to, 130–131,
    138–139
Six Sigma, 151–152. *See also*
    Lean Six Sigma; Six Sigma
    statistical tool finder matrix;
    3 sigma process; Traditional
    Six Sigma
  businesses using, 3
  classes in, 23
  concepts of, 4
  design of, 165
  goal of, 5
  history of, 4–5
  methodology, 171
  regression analysis used by, 40
  simplified gauge verification in,
    72–73
  statistics of, 61
  teams in, 6
  titles of, 5–6
  tools, 9
  traditional FMEA in, 23

Six Sigma (*Cont.*)
  traditional process flow diagram
    for, 35
  training in, 10
Six Sigma statistical tool finder
  matrix, 167–168
Skewed distribution, 151
Software development
  data for, 54
  fishbone diagrams for, 32
  histograms for, 93
  nonnormal distributions for, 150
  probability in, 84
  proportional data for, 141
  simplified FMEA for, 24
  simplified process flow diagrams
    for, 35
  simplified QFD for, 17
  time plots for, 41
  variables data for, 116
Specification
  limit, 160
  of master, 75
  of problems, 66–67
  upper/lower, 59
Stacked parts, 165–166
Standard deviation, 118, 170
Standardized normal distribution
  table, 101
  process comparison with, 152
  use on normal process, 99
  Z value in, 99–105
Statistics. *See also* The Six Sigma
  statistical tool finder matrix
  analysis of, 50, 108
  esoteric, 153
  proportional data for, 140–142
  of Six Sigma, 61
  terminology of, 139
Symmetry, 103

Taylorism. *See* Scientific management
Teams, 6
Terminology, 139
Tests. *See also* Chi-square test;
  Correlation tests; F test; T-test

of confidence, 140
for performance, 122–123
of sensitivity, 146
variables data, 115–116
visual correlation, 40–41
3 sigma process, 60–61
Time plots
  construction of, 41
  of variables, 43–44
Tolerance
  allowable, 59
  limit to, 160
  need-based, 170
  process variation compared to, 62
  RSS, 165–166
Toyota, 5, 35
Traditional control chart, 158
Traditional FMEA
  simplified FMEA v., 28
  in Six Sigma, 23
Traditional process flow diagram
  on computers, 37
  for Six Sigma, 35
Traditional QFD
  components of, 21–23
  simplified QFD v., 22–23
Traditional Six Sigma, 34
  lean manufacturing from, 5
  simplified process flow diagram
    for, 38
Training
  cross, 83
  in Six Sigma, 10
Trends, 160–161
T-test, 140
  simplified t distribution table
    compared to, 129–130,
    137–138
  variables data and, 172
Two-tailed problems, 121

Uniform distribution, 152

Value. *See also* Z value
  of bin edge in histogram, 94
  of sigma, 97

Variables
  combination of, 164
  minimizing, 66
  sigma on, 117
  time plots of, 43–44
Variables data, 49, 75, 172
  attribute data v., 144
  measurement resolution of, 50
  proportional data v., 141
  regularity of, 159
  sample size on, 120–124, 171
  simplified gauge verification used
    on, 171
  testing for, 115–116
  t-test and, 172
Variation. *See also* Process variation
  of data, 58

in gauge reading, 72
in process, 59, 62, 67–69, 158
reduction in, 66
Vertical feedback bar, 159–160
Visual correlation tests, 40–41,
  45, 125. *See also* Correlation
  tests
VOC. *See* Voice of the customer
Voice of the customer (VOC), 15

X successes. *See* Numbers s

Z value, 106, 108
  accuracy of, 107
  probability related to, 121
  in standardized normal
    distribution table, 99–105

ABOUT THE AUTHOR

Warren Brussee was an engineer and plant manager at General Electric for 33 years. He is the holder of multiple patents for his Six Sigma work and is the author of numerous Six Sigma books, including *Statistics for Six Sigma Made Easy* and *All About Six Sigma*. He lives in Columbia, SC.